AYATULLAH IBRAHIM AMINI

An Introduction to Islam

First published by Ansariyan Publications 2020

Copyright © 2020 by Ayatullah Ibrahim Amini

All rights reserved. No part of this publication may be reproduced, stored or transmitted in any form or by any means, electronic, mechanical, photocopying, recording, scanning, or otherwise without written permission from the publisher. It is illegal to copy this book, post it to a website, or distribute it by any other means without permission.

First edition

Translation by Sayyid Athar Husain S. H. Rizvi

Contents

Part I: Principles of Religion	1
Part II: Morals and manners in Islam	25
Part III: Islam and Faith	49
Part IV: Man in viewpoint of Islam	82
Part V: Duties, laws and their sources	103
Part VI: Branches of Religion (Furu Deen)	149
Bibliography	204

Part I: Principles of Religion

Principles of Faith

Principles of Faith

*I*slamic subjects and problems can be divided into two groups: Principles of faith (Usul Deen) and secondary issues (Furu Deen). Principles of faith (Usul Deen) are also called as beliefs and secondary issues (Furu Deen) are known as duties. Secondary issues (Furu Deen) are duties and dos and don'ts, which are imposed by the Almighty God on man and they can be divided into three groups: Ethics, worship acts and non-worship laws. The last is also called as 'dealings' (Maamilaat).

Principles of faith (Usul Deen) are regarded as pillars of Islam and faith on them is necessary for a person if he wants to be considered a Muslim. They are: belief in oneness of God, resurrection and prophethood of Prophet Muhammad (s).

However, Shia Imamiyah, in addition to these consider faith in Imamate also as part of fundamentals of belief, which in terminology is known as Principles of Religion.

Principles of belief are also called as 'world view'. It is such a view that man has a sense of responsibility towards the creator of the universe and accepts the divine duties, which have been arranged to guarantee success in the world and hereafter. Laws and duties are called as 'ideology'.

Matters of beliefs are divided into two groups: Roots and branches. Fundamentals of belief are matters, which are necessary to believe in if the faith of a person is to be considered true; like Oneness of God, Resurrection and Prophethood.

However, the branches of beliefs are derived from the fundamentals, like: Divine names, Positive Attributes (Sifaat Thubutiyyah) and Negative Attributes (Sifaat Salbiyyah), Infallibility of prophets, intercession, purgatory (Barzakh), process of enlivening of the dead and such other matters.

Role of beliefs in success of man

Principles of religion and world view can affect the success of man from the following aspects:

A) Dos and don'ts, which affect the lifestyle of man and which are derived from his world view and special beliefs.

B) Obtaining recognition of the facts; especially the recognition of Almighty Allah, from the point of view of Islam is a personal value; on the contrary it is considered among the best of worship acts and which causes perfection of self and proximity to God. Knowledge and recognition directly affects the self of man and convey it to perfection.

On the basis of this, obtaining recognition and knowledge is introduced in Quran as a great and valuable worship act.

"Allah is He Who created seven heavens, and of the earth the like of them; the decree continues to descend among them, that you may know that Allah has power over all

things and that Allah indeed encompasses all things in (His) knowledge." (65:12)

In the same way, it says:

"Allah will exalt those of you who believe, and those who are given knowledge, in high degrees; and Allah is Aware of what you do." (58:11)

Amirul Momineen (a) said: O believer, knowledge and manners are values of your self, thus make efforts in gaining knowledge, as much as your knowledge and manners increase, your status and value would also increase, because through knowledge you would be guided to your Lord and through manners you would be able to serve the Lord in the best way and one who has good manners, would become eligible for the guardianship (Wilayat) and proximity of God. Hence, accept good advice, so that you may be saved from the punishment of God.[1]

Imam Ja'far Sadiq (a) said: "The best worship acts are knowledge of God and submission before Him."[2]

Hisham bin Hakam has narrated from Imam Musa Kazim (a) that he said: O Hisham, God deputed the prophets as His messengers to make the people wise and mindful of God. The more they accept and believe in these messengers, the greater is their God-consciousness. The wisest among men is one that is more knowledgeable about; and one that is most perfect in his reasoning enjoys the highest status among men in this life and the life hereafter.[2]

C) Belief in God in the possibility of proving the intention of proximity and sincerity is among conditions of worship and is the

---

[1] *Biharul Anwar*, Vol. 1, Pg. 180

[2] *Al-Kafi*, Vol. 1, Pg. 16

real secret of gaining of proximity. If belief on God is not there and deeds are not performed for Him, it will not have value and eligibility of rewards of the hereafter.

Ways of recognition

Islam considers gaining of recognition and knowledge to be possible for man, therefore in Quran man is invited to contemplate on the amazing aspects of the earth, skies, mountains, seas, trees, animals, sun, creation of night and day and other matters. Now if gaining of recognition had not been possible, call to study, contemplation and thought would have been absurd.

Now we shall explain what recognition and obtaining of knowledge is:

1. Senses: Man can maintain connection with the external world and understand things through the sense of sight, hearing, taste, smell and touch. However, these senses only perceive material things and they cannot perceive abstract matters; that is they don't have the power to perceive and see the angels and Almighty Allah directly; although these senses can be mediums of recognizing the creator of the world.

2. Mind and intellect: The best way to perceive reality and to gain certainty is through use of reason and logical argumentation. Quran invites man to contemplate on the amazing aspects of creation so that in this way he may discover the creator of the world and His knowledge and power.

The Holy Quran says:

"Say: Consider what is it that is in the heavens and the earth; and signs and warners do not avail a people who would not believe."

It also says:

> *"Have they not traveled in the land so that they should have hearts with which to understand, or ears with which to hear? For surely it is not the eyes that are blind, but blind are the hearts which are in the breasts."* (22:46)

Not only has the Holy Quran urged man to contemplate, it itself makes use of logical reasonings to prove some of its points; like when it says:

> *"If there had been in them any gods except Allah, they would both have certainly been in a state of disorder; therefore glory be to Allah, the Lord of the dominion, above what they attribute (to Him)."* (21:22)

And it says:

> *"Never did Allah take to Himself a son, and never was there with him any (other) god - in that case would each god have certainly taken away what he created, and some of them would certainly have overpowered others; glory be to Allah above what they describe!* (23:91)

The Holy Prophet of Islam (s) and the Holy Imams (a) were also people of reasoning. Sometimes they resorted to logical reasoning in order to prove roots of religion. They didn't ask their opponents to 'just shut up'; on the contrary, they tried to prove to them the facts through reasoning and discussions. Discussions of the Prophet and Imams are nicely recorded in history.

On the basis of this it can be said that: Islam is a religion of logic and reasoning and it accepts reason as a reliable instrument and has called its followers towards it. However, the correct conclusion for reason and logical sources has special conditions and its application is also within particular limits.

3. Purification of self and cleaning of conscience: One of the methods of understanding facts and discovering realities is purification of self and cleansing of conscience. With regard to this, they say: The soul of man is an ethereal and abstract element having the capability to witness some of realities of the unseen world without traversing the path of reasoning. That which obstructs this perception is the filthiness of the soul due to sins and material relations. Thus if man adopts piety, cleans his self from sins, reduces worldly relations and bestows luminosity to his self and performs worship and remembrance of God, he can become eligible for divine grace and he would perceive the realities. Scholars have argued from some verses and traditions in order to prove the correctness of this method:

The Holy Quran says:

> *"And the soul and Him Who made it perfect. Then He inspired it to understand what is right and wrong for it. He will indeed be successful who purifies it. And he will indeed fail who corrupts it." (91:7-10)*

And it says:

> *"O you who believe! If you are careful of (your duty to) Allah, He will grant you a distinction and do away with your evils and forgive you; and Allah is the Lord of mighty grace." (8:29)*

On the basis of this, purification and discipline of the soul is a desired act, which becomes the cause of his success and perfection. If man observes piety and does not smear his soul with sins, he would reach a level when he can see the realities and distinguish between truth and falsehood.

"The Messenger of Allah (s) has also said: One who devotes himself solely to Almighty Allah for forty days and nights, springs of wisdom from his heart would flow on his tongue."[3]

Amirul Momineen (a) said: "Hearts of pure persons are eligible for attention of Almighty Allah, so one who purifies his heart would earn the attention of Almighty Allah."[4]

Imam Ali (a) also said: "Glad tidings to one who performs worship acts and supplications only for Almighty Allah and does not make his heart involved in that which his eyes see and does not make that which reaches his ears to forget the remembrance of God and is not aggrieved by that which is given to others."[5]

Lady Fatima Zahra (s) said: One who sends his sincere worship acts to Almighty Allah, Allah also sends to him the best of the interests."[6]

It can be concluded from these verses and traditions that the way of obtaining knowledge is not restricted to reasoning and evidence, on the contrary there is another way, which in other words is: Purification and discipline of the soul from sins, bad morals and endeavor in worship and sincerity of actions for Allah. Realities can be reached from this path also.

Some divine saints and sincere people in order to gain knowledge and certainty have traversed this path and have reached the aim, but traversing this path is extremely difficult and is not possible by all, because it requires struggle (Jihad) with the self, and abstinence.

---

[3] *Biharul Anwar*, Vol. 70, Pg. 242

[4] *Ghurarul Hikam wa Durarul Kalam*, Pg. 501

[5] *Biharul Anwar*, Vol. 70, Pg. 229

[6] *Biharul Anwar*, Vol. 70, Pg. 249

4. Information given by prophets and Infallible Imams (a): Though Islam invites people to contemplate and take benefit from reasoning and considers it to be a sensual value, but the custom of the prophets was not as such that they always invited to method of reasoning, on the contrary mostly they took advantage of their truthfulness and honesty and invited people to faith. When the trustworthy and truthful Prophet of Islam said to people: I invite you to faith in Allah and monotheism, you are not annihilated by death, on the contrary you are transferred to the world of the hereafter, so that you may see the rewards for your good deeds and punishment of your bad deeds, most people gained faith through his statements. Mostly the call was not accompanied with reasonings, but his statements brought faith and certainty. Although such a faith was not defective and baseless, rather it was stronger than the faith derived through logical reasonings.

These people as a result of the reliance they had on the Prophet of Islam considered his information to be definite and developed belief on its correctness and brought faith in it. Although if an individual or some individuals demanded evidence, he convinced them through reasoning and was even fond of it; but such was not his usual style.

On the basis of this, the above style can also be regarded as one of the ways of obtaining knowledge, certainty and faith, which was employed by the prophets.

5. Inculcation of parents and teacher: Faith of many people is created through inculcation by father, mother or teacher. Guardians and nurturers prepare the child with the word of God; after that they mention the roots of religion to him in ordinary manner and read them out to him till he memorizes them perfectly and they make it appealing to him. Then they teach him recitation of 'Hamd'[7] and other Surahs, method of ablution (Wudhu) and ritual prayers.

---

[7] First chapter of the Holy Quran

Gradually the child develops faith in God, Prophet and resurrection and grows up with this same faith and belief. Reading books of religious teachings also strengthens faith. Although some of them, when they grow up investigate this and strengthen their childhood faith through reasonings and proofs, but most remain content with their childhood faith and also have no doubt, because in proving faith resolve and certainty is the condition and they possessed it.

As for faith, which is based on contemplation and reasonings, it has precedence over inculcated faith, but it is not that if it had been without investigation and reasoning, it would have harmed actual faith.

Now, if a person is having doubt in one of the principles of belief, he should logically search it out and make his faith stable. Shortcoming and carelessness in this matter is not allowed.

However, with regard to secondary beliefs one can rest content with conjectural reasonings like solitary reports (Khabar Wahid); although investigation and acquisition of certainty in secondary beliefs is also when possible, having precedence over conjectural reasoning.

Station of Mastership (Wilayat) in Islam

Station of Mastership (Wilayat) in Islam

Since Wilayat has a fundamental and distinctive role in Islamic teachings, we would have a brief discussion about it here.

Wilayat is introduced in traditions to be the most important pillar of Islam. Imam Muhammad Baqir (a) said: Islam is based on five pillars: Prayer, Zakat, Fast, Hajj and Wilayat. People are not invited to anything with as much emphasis, as they are invited to Wilayat.[8]

---

[8] Al-Kafi, Vol. 1, Pg. 18

In another tradition, Zurarah says: I asked Imam Baqir (a): "Which of these five is the most important?" He replied: "Wilayat is the most important, because it is their key. The Guardian is a guide to them."⁹

Wilayat is in the meaning of guardianship and taking charge of affairs of others. The world of 'Wali' is also from the same root and it describes one in charge of guardianship of an individual or individuals, like Wali of the young and Wali of the mentally challenged persons. The word of 'Waali' is also derived from the same root. The governor or governor-general is called as 'Waali' since the administration of the city and affairs of citizens are in his charge and they are supposed to obey his commands. The Holy Prophet (s) also has the same type of Wilayat over the Ummah, since he is their guardian and has discretion over them. Almighty Allah says in Quran:

"The Prophet has a greater claim on the faithful than they have on themselves..." (33:6)

The word of Maula is also derived from the same root. That is why the Holy Prophet (s), at the beginning of Ghadeer sermon in Farewell Hajj addressed the people: Do I not have more authority on you more than what you have on yourself? They said: Why not? Then he said: Of whomsoever I am the master; this Ali is also his master.¹⁰

Umar bin Khattab, who was present in the event of Ghadeer and witnessed the appointment of Ali (a), also derived the same meaning from the word of 'Maula', because he remarked to Ali (a): "O Ali, congratulations; you have become the master of every believer man

---

⁹ Al-Kafi, Vol. 1, Pg. 18
10

and woman."[11]

It can be concluded from these statements that Wilayat is an executive position and not only a holy rank.

Wilayat during the lifetime of the Holy Prophet

Now the question arises that what were the circumstances of Muslims during the proclamation of prophethood (Besat) of the Prophet of Islam (s)? Did they live without leaders and social administrator? Or an arrangement, control and rulership existed although in a limited way and in enforcing simple laws? In order to get the replies to these questions, it is necessary to cast a brief glance on the rules and laws of Islam:

Laws of Islam, which are mentioned in Quran and traditions, can all be divided into two types:

A) Individual laws and duties like Prayers, fast, Hajj, observing good manners, refraining from bad morals, purification, impurity and other individual laws.

Such laws are personal duties and they are addressed to each and every duty bound person individually and acting on them does not require presence of rulership and social management.

B) The second type of laws and political duties – are social, like: Struggle (Jihad) to propagate Islam, defending existence of Islam and Muslims, military preparedness, securing social peace, legal judgment and solving of disputes, enforcing penalties, blood monies and retaliations, punishment of criminals, mutual relations between Islamic countries, relations with others, collection of Zakat and its proper use, collection of Khums and its proper use, and tens of other similar social matters. Such social and political laws and rules have are also included in Islam. With a little consideration, we would know that acting on such laws needs formation of institutions headed by a

---

[11] *Tohafful Uqul*, Pg. 383

determined and a religious ruler and leader.

That is why it can be said that rulership and Wilayat is included in religion and there should always be a ruler who is in charge of guaranteeing the application of political and social laws. And if it is not so, a great part of Islamic laws would be in suspended condition.

The Holy Prophet; the first Wali of Muslims

Although in Quran we don't have a verse in which the Messenger of Allah (s) has clearly ordered formation of government, but in some verses he has commanded about some practices and acts, which are concerned with government; for example the following verses can be cited as proof:

> *"Surely We have revealed the Book to you with the truth that you may judge between people by means of that which Allah has taught you; and be not an advocate on behalf of the treacherous." (4:105)*

> *"And We have revealed to you the Book with the truth, verifying what is before it of the Book and a guardian over it, therefore judge between them by what Allah has revealed, and do not follow their low desires (to turn away) from the truth that has come to you..." (5:48)*

> *"O Prophet! Strive hard against the unbelievers and the hypocrites and be unyielding to them." (9:73)*

> *"O Prophet! urge the believers to war..." (8:65)*

> *"Take alms out of their property, you would cleanse them and purify them thereby..." (9:103)*

It is clear that arbitration and solving disputes of people, encouraging people to Jihad, collection of Zakat and taxes and expending them in the specific ways are from the duties of the ruler, and since their performance was asked from the Messenger of Allah (s), it is known that he was ruler appointed by Almighty Allah. Therefore, it must be said: The Prophet of Islam in addition to receiving revelation, its protection and propagation to people, also had other duties and it implies formation of government, enforcing of political and social laws, leadership and administration of Islamic Ummah in different matters.

The Holy Prophet (s) in managing the affairs of Islamic state, took advantage of laws, which he received through revelation; he was also authorized to issue commands and apply them in accordance with exigency of the nation. Such laws were named as laws of governance. Muslims also are duty bound to obey his commands.

The Holy Quran says:

> *"O you who believe! obey Allah and obey the Apostle and those in authority from among you; then if you quarrel about anything, refer it to Allah and the Apostle, if you believe in Allah and the last day; this is better and very good in the end." (4:59)*

It can be concluded from this verse that it is obligatory on the believers to obey the commands of three persons: Allah, the glorified, the Prophet and those vested with authority (Ulil Amr). Obedience of Allah is in the instances when the Prophet announces the command as revelation and message of God. Obedience of the Prophet is in instances, when he issues commands in the capacity of religious authority and ruler of Muslims and not as divine revelation. Such laws are called laws of government and authority. The third type is obedience of Ulil Amr. Ulil Amr is one who is introduced by the Prophet as a ruler and owner of authority. In many traditions, the Holy Imams (a), who are from Ahle Bayt (a) and progeny of the Holy Prophet (s) are introduced as implications of Ulil Amr. They are also having authority on people and their obedience is obligatory. With reference to books of biography, it would become absolutely clear that the Holy Prophet of Islam since the beginning of the migration (Hijra) to Medina and when the call to Islam became evident, felt the need of establishing a government, which would protect the interests of Islam and Muslims and when he got opportunity, he took the necessary steps. During a period of ten years in Medina, gradually he performed actions, which were necessary to form a simple government and to administer a limited society. Some of them are as follows:

Selection of minister and advisor, selection or appointment of chief and governor for big and small towns, selection of judge, establishment of courts of justice, selection of persons for application of penalties, guarding the prisons and prisoners, selection of chiefs of tribes, selection of persons for gathering information and intelligence, selection of persons to enjoin good and forbid evil, establishment of classes for Quranic education, writing, jurisprudence and laws, selection of individuals for making copies of Quran, selecting individuals to write letters, selecting officials and collectors of Zakat, individuals for collecting taxes, treasurer and treasury in charge, accountants, officials for paying and distributing shares, appointment of commander-in-chief, standard bearer, weapons in charge, selection of security personnel, supervisor of commercial transactions, and other small and big posts of responsibilities.[12] Such types of acts are definitely from the ranks of rulership. On the basis of this, one should not reject the rulership of the Prophet of Islam. He was the first owner of authority (Wali Amr) over Muslims and the founder of the Islamic government, and his Wilayat is proved from revelation and Quran. It should be mentioned that although the position of Wilayat and rulership was given to His Eminence by God, it would not have been possibly realized externally without earnestness, loyalty, sacrifice and preparations through people. From this aspect, responsibility of application of social and political laws of Islam in Quran is placed directly upon the Muslims. For example, Almighty Allah says in the Holy Quran:

"And strive hard in (the way of) Allah, (such) a striving as is due to Him..." (22:78)

"And fight in the way of Allah with those who fight with you, and do not exceed the limits, surely Allah does not love those who exceed the limits." (2:190)

"..And fight the polytheists all together as they fight you all together..." (9:36)

"And prepare against them what force you can and horses tied at the frontier, to frighten thereby the enemy of Allah and your enemy..." (8:60)

---

[12] Refer: Shaykh Abdul Haqq Kattani, At-Tarateebul Idariya

"And (as for) the man who steals and the woman who steals, cut off their hands as a punishment for what they have earned, an exemplary punishment from Allah..." (5:38)

"(As for) the fornicatress and the fornicator, flog each of them, (giving) a hundred stripes..." (24:2)

"And from among you there should be a party who invite to good and enjoin what is right and forbid the wrong..." (3:104)

"O you who believe! Be maintainers of justice, bearers of witness of Allah's sake..." (4:135)

"O you who believe! do not take the unbelievers for friends rather than the believers; do you desire that you should give to Allah a manifest proof against yourselves?" (4:144)

"O you who believe! do not take the Jews and the Christians for friends; they are friends of each other." (5:51)

"You are the best of the nations raised up for (the benefit of) men; you enjoin what is right and forbid the wrong and

believe in Allah..." (3:110)

From the above verses, which are revealed about the 'obligatory-ness' of holy struggle (Jihad) and defense, military preparedness, application of punishments and fines, enjoining good and forbidding evil, obligatoryness of establishment of social justice, relations of Muslims with others and tens of other similar verses and hundreds of traditions, which are recorded with reference to jurisprudence, political, administrative, economic, dissemination of sciences and popularizing of cultural values and prevention of opposing values, can be nicely concluded that the holy lawmaker of Islam has regarded Muslims to be a proper nation, which should, in order to administer its community and to fulfill its social and political needs, form organizations. And since Muslims have practically accepted the leadership and Wilayat of the Holy Prophet (s) the possibility of formation of government for him is obtained.

Wilayat after the Messenger of Allah (s)

After the passing away of the Holy Prophet (s), although divine revelation (direct contact with Allah and receiving of laws) came to an end, the religion was perfected and legislation of laws reached its conclusion, but with attention to the fact that the Prophet of Islam is the last of the prophets and the religion of Islam is a universal religion and it is to endure till Judgment Day and would always remain as a torch of guidance, it is necessary that after the passing away of the Messenger of Allah (s) there should be a prominent person to take over his responsibilities and pursue his agenda. He is named as the Caliph of the Prophet and the Imam of Muslims.

The Holy Prophet bore the following four responsibilities:
1. Receipt of divine laws and messages through revelation. 2. Conveyance of divine messages to people. 3. Protection of divine laws.

4. Formation of government and enforcement of political and social laws of Islam. In all these stages, the Holy Prophet (s) was infallible from sins and doubts. In books of theology, it is proved that the Caliph of the Prophet also like him should be immune from mistakes, doubts and forgetfulness so that aims of the Prophet should be pursued and the true religion remains strong.

Imamite Shia, with attention to the need of condition of infallibility in Caliph say: Except for the Prophet, no one can introduce and appoint the Caliph, as except for the Prophet, who is having divine revelation, no one else is aware of the infallibles.

From the same argument and numerous historical evidences and tens of traditions that are present in sources of narrations, it is said: The Messenger of Allah (s) due to his concern for survival of Islam and its spread and greatness of Islamic Ummah was definitely not oblivious of appointing his infallible successor.

Therefore historical testimonies and traditions hint at that great personage during the period of his prophethood and he was always concerned about this important matter and for this purpose had selected Ali Ibne Abi Talib (a). He paid utmost attention to his education and training and entrusted necessary knowledges to him. Imam Ali (a) also with his personal capacity and with divine supports memorized the knowledges and did not forget anything. Moreover, as per the orders of the Prophet, he wrote down all knowledges to leave behind for the Imams succeeding him.

Imam Ali (a), as a result of the special bestowals of the Messenger of Allah (s) mastered all the sciences of prophethood. As the Holy Prophet (s) mentioned about him: I am the city of knowledge and Ali is its gate; so one who wants to seek knowledge should come to its gate,[13] and tens of other traditions, which are recorded in books of Shia and Ahle

---

[13] Mustadrak, Hakim Nishapuri, Vol. 3, Pg. 126

Sunnat.

The aim of the Messenger of Allah (s) in stating the excellences and virtues of Imam Ali (a) was to prepare public opinion and prepare the grounds of his introduction and appointment as his successor and for Imamate of Muslims and always looking for opportunity to declare his appointment formally.

These circumstances continued till the 10th year of Hijrat. That year, the Holy Prophet (s) decided to perform the Hajj of the Holy House of Kaaba. He invited all Muslims to participate in the Hajj so that they may witness the rituals of Hajj from close quarters. The Messenger of Allah (s) intended to officially declare the appointment of Ali Ibne Abi Talib (a) as his successor and to introduce him to the pilgrims, who had arrived from various countries to perform the Hajj. The rituals of Hajj came to an end and the pilgrims started returning to their hometowns. When the Messenger of Allah (s) and his followers reached Ghadeer Khum it was almost noon and the climate was extremely hot. At that moment Jibraeel arrived with the following verse:

"O Apostle! deliver what has been revealed to you from your Lord; and if you do it not, then you have not delivered His message, and Allah will protect you from the people; surely Allah will not guide the unbelieving people." (5:67)

The Holy Prophet (s) halted at that spot. He issued orders to prepare that place for Noon Prayer. Pilgrims gathered. After the prayer, the Messenger of Allah (s) mounted the pulpit. He recited a lengthy sermon, which later came to be known as tradition of Ghadeer Khum. This tradition is reported in various versions and is present in reliable Shia and Sunni sources. Below we mention one such version:

Zaid bin Arqam says: When the Messenger of Allah (s) was returning from the Farewell Hajj he reached Ghadeer Khum. Initially he ordered them to sweep the ground below the trees and then he delivered a sermon: As if I have been called to Allah. I leave among you two important things by way of trust and one of them is greater than another: The Book of Allah (Quran) and my progeny. Try to take care of these two trusts. They would not separate from each other till Judgment Day. Then he said: Allah, the Mighty and Sublime is my master and I am the master of all believers. Then he raised the hand of Ali (a) and said: Of whomsoever I am the master, this Ali is also his master.

O Allah, take under Your guardianship whoever accepts the mastership (Wilayat) of Ali and be inimical to whoever is inimical to Ali.[14]

Baraa Ibne Azib has added the following words in narrating the same sermon that in the beginning the Messenger of Allah (s) asked: Am I not having more authority over the believer than they have on themselves? They replied: Why not, O Messenger of Allah (s)? You are having more authority. At that moment he pointed to Ali and said: Of whomsoever I am the master, this Ali is also his master.[15]

After that Umar Ibne Khattab met Ali (a) and said: "Congratulations Ali, you have become my master and the master of all believer men and women."[16]

The tradition of Ghadeer is a widely related (Mutawatir) and authentic tradition and there is no doubt in its authenticity.

Thus on that blessed day, the Holy Prophet (s) performed two most important tasks: One was that he declared Quran and Progeny to be complimentaries of each other and left them as two reliable sources of reference for the Muslims as trusts and advised them to refer to them

---

[14] Mustadrak, Hakim Nishapuri, Vol. 3, Pg. 119; Bidaya wan Nihaya, Vol. 3, Pg. 228

[15] Al-Bidaya wan Nihaya, Vol. 3, Pg. 229

[16] Al-Bidaya wan Nihaya, Vol. 3, Pg. 229

to derive the laws of religion.

Another was introduction of Ali Ibne Abi Talib (a) as master and owner of discretion. In this act he delegated to him the position of his Wilayat and rulership so that he may become the Caliph and Imam of Muslims after him; and that by enforcing the laws of religion about whom he was perfectly knowledgeable, he should administer the Islamic dominions.[17]

On the basis of this, the Messenger of Allah (s) in the tradition of Ghadeer and other traditions transferred three of his duties to Ali Ibne Abi Talib (a): 1. Protection of divine laws. 2. Conveying them to Muslims. 3. Rulership and enforcement of political and social laws of Islam; as he was one of the implications of 'progeny' and Ahle Bayt (a).

From the tradition of Ghadeer and tens of similar traditions, it can well be concluded that with the death of the Messenger of Allah (s) the period of his rule has not ended and enforcement of political and social laws of Islam do not remain without an infallible executive. On the contrary, by appointment and nomination of Ali (a), he fixed the duration of the Imamate of the infallible Imams.

Imam Ali (a), as per the orders of the Holy Prophet (s) during his lifetime, appointed Imam Hasan (a) and Imam Hasan (a) appointed his brother, Imam Husain (a) and Imam Husain (a) appointed his son, Imam Ali Ibne Husain (a) to Imamate and in this way Imamate continued till the twelfth Imam.

According to belief of Shia Imamiyah, after the Messenger of Allah (s) the following twelve have been appointed as Caliphs and Imams in sequence:

Ali Ibne Abi Talib (a)
Hasan Ibne Ali (a)
Husain Ibne Ali (a)

---

[17] Refer: Allamah Amini, Al-Ghadeer and Ibrahim Amini, Algohai Fazeelat

Ali Ibne Husain (a)
Muhammad Ibne Ali (a)
Ja'far Ibne Muhammad (a)
Musa Ibne Ja'far (a)
Ali Ibne Musa (a)
Muhammad Ibne Ali (a)
Ali Ibne Muhammad (a)
Hasan Ibne Ali (a)
Hujjat Ibnul Hasan al-Askari (a)

Imamate and Caliphate of these twelve personages in its own capacity is proved through evidence and proofs.[18]

Each of the above mentioned personages were having the two necessary qualifications of Imamate: (1) Infallibility from mistakes, forgetfulness and sins; and (2) knowledge of all the laws of Shariah. That is why they were directly appointed by the Holy Prophet (s) as Imams.

Although except for Ali Ibne Abi Talib (a) and that also after a delay and only for few years, none of them practically reached to the post of Caliphate, but the Caliphate of the Messenger of Allah (s) was their right, which due to ignorance and shortcoming of people in defending Wilayat was trespassed and Caliphate deviated from the path that the Holy Prophet (s) had specified for it. Muslims were duty bound and are duty bound to have faith in Wilayat of the Infallible Imams from the progeny of Prophet and they should make efforts to prepare grounds for the rule of the righteous and to become aloof from the rule of non-righteous. This is in fact the implication of Tawalla and Tabarra.[19]

---

[18] Refer: Hurre Amili, Asbatul Huda; Sayyid Muhammad Hadi Milani, Qadatana; Ibrahim Amini, Algohai Fazeelat

[19] Tawalla means to love Allah and everything and everyone associated with Him and Tabarra means to be aloof from the enemy of Allah and enemy of everything related to Him.

Wilayat during the period of Occultation

As concluded from a large number of traditions, the authority (Wali Amr) of Muslims is the twelfth Imam, His Eminence, Mahdi (a), who has attained this position from Almighty Allah and through the Messenger of Allah (s) and the Holy Imams (a). But due to the shortcoming of people in preparing the prefaces of his reappearance and establishment of his rule, he is compelled to live in occultation and is in anticipation of the time, which would provide the background of his reappearance, but in this time also the holy lawmaker of Islam (God) has not ignored the enforcement of His social and political laws and establishment of Islamic rule.

Since Muslims during the period of the Messenger of Allah (s) and during the tenure of infallible Imams are duty bound to make efforts and struggle in establishment of their kingdom and to prepare the background of reaching the position of Wilayat, during the time of occultation also, they are duty bound to recognize the most superior of the people; that they accept their leadership, obey their commands and prepare background for enforcement of all Islamic laws and religious rules and regulations. Such persons would be authority (Wali Amr) and representatives of the Imam of the Time (a) and their Wilayat would have the same status as that of the Holy Imam (a) and the Holy Prophet (s). But how and in what manner can one obtain these qualifications is a matter, which requires extensive research and study. In this regard, a large number of traditions have been recorded from the Holy Imams (a), which can be found in reliable sources and they can help us to decide this matter.

In this book, it is not practically possible to study this important subject in detail. But many scholars have published well researched books on this topic; especially after the Islamic revolution (of Iran).

However, in brief, we can say that the authority (Wali Amr) and leader of Muslims should have the following qualities:

1. Academic capability to issue verdicts in various subjects of jurisprudence.
2. Justice and piety, which is necessary for leadership of the community.
3. Right political and social opinion, management, determination and sufficient ability for leadership.

Part II: Morals and manners in Islam

Morals and Manners in Islam

'Khulq' means a good disposition and personal behavior. The late scholar, Faiz Kashani defines morals thus: Disposition is an aspect, which has become deeply rooted in the soul of man, in such a way that easily and without any need of thinking and contemplating acts are committed by him. Thus if from that aspect such acts are committed by him, which are logically and religiously praiseworthy that aspect is called as a good disposition and if acts are evil, the disposition is called as bad.[20]

Intellectuals, in defining moral acts, have said: Act or quality is a value, whose good or evil is detected by perfect reason and all human beings, at all times and places are having consensus on its goodness or evil. Moral act is an act that realization can perceive its goodness and the duty of man itself sees that it should be performed, or it perceives its evil and personally feels that its performance does not befit his humanity and it should be abandoned.

Good character in Islam is having great status and lofty position. So

---

[20] Haqaiq, Pg. 54

much so that it is considered to be a sign of perfection of faith. Good character is described as the heaviest act that would be placed in the scale of deeds. Development of good morals was so important that it was said to be the aim of the sending of the Prophet.

The Holy Quran says:Ia l

> ***"Certainly Allah conferred a benefit upon the believers when He raised among them an Apostle from among themselves, reciting to them His communications and purifying them, and teaching them the Book and the wisdom, although before that they were surely in manifest error." (3:164)***

The Messenger of Allah (s) said: I advise you to adopt good morals, because Allah, the Mighty and Sublime has sent me with this aim.[21]

The Holy Prophet said: I have been sent to perfect morals.[22]

Imam Muhammad Baqir (a) said: The most perfect of the believers are those whose morals are the best.[23]

The Messenger of Allah (s) said: On Judgment Day, nothing would be placed on the scale of deeds more valuable than good nature.[24]

Imam Ja'far Sadiq (a) said: Allah, the Mighty would reward a servant for good morals with such reward, which is given day and night to the fighter in the way of Allah.[25]

The Holy Prophet (s) said: Good moral is half the faith.[26]

---

[21] Biharul Anwar, Vol. 69, Pg. 375

[22] Mustadrakul Wasail, Vol. 11, Pg. 187

[23] Al-Kafi, Vol. 2, Pg. 100

[24] Al-Kafi, Vol. 2, Pg. 99

[25] Al-Kafi, Vol. 2, Pg. 100

[26] Mishkatul Anwar, Pg. 223

Islam had advised much with regard to purification and discipline of self and development of good character. A large number of verses of Quran are with regard to moral science, so much so that most stories of Quran pursue moral aims. Thousands of traditions of the Holy Prophet (s) and the Holy Imams (a) have been narrated on the topic of good and bad morals. Glad tidings for adopting a good character and punishments of smearing oneself with bad morals which are mentioned are definitely not less than that which is mentioned about the obligatory and prohibited acts, because they can either lead one to the perfection of self and proximity to Allah or decline of self and remoteness from God.

On the basis of this, ethical matters should be considered at par with Islamic laws or higher and one cannot be shortcoming and careless in observing them under the pretext that they are ethical commands. Basically, human life is not possible without good morals; therefore every nation and community of the world followed ethical matters and does so even today.

Moral affects success and comfort or misfortune and restlessness in two ways:

A: Worldly life and community living: If individuals of a society are aware of their duties, they fulfill rights of each other, they are kind and concerned for each other, they are having cooperation in good deeds, they hasten to solve the difficulties of each other and in one word it can be said that they consider success and comfort of society as success and comfort of themselves, they have a happy and healthy life and as much as possible, they take advantage of worldly bounties.

On the contrary, if they were not bound by ethical restraints, they would not have got their comforts. Therefore, success or misfortune of a society should be searched in observance of restraint in ethical criteria or lack of it in its individuals. That is why Islam has emphasized too much on adoption of social ethics.

The Messenger of Allah (s) said: Success of man lies in good morals and his misfortune lies in bad morals.[27]

Imam Ja'far Sadiq (a) said: No life is more pleasing than good morals.[28]

In the same way, he said: Good behavior increases sustenance.[29]

And he said: Good manners and morals populate towns and increase lifespans.[30]

He also said: One who is having bad morals is putting himself in hardship and punishment.[31]

We have a large number of traditions with regard to social manners and communal behavior, which are recorded in books like: Biharul Anwar, Vols. 74 and 75; Al-Kafi, Vol. 2; Jami Ahadith Shia, Wasailush Shia etc.

B: Spiritual perfection or decline: Good morals give perfection to the self and bring man close to God. Bad morals also cause decline and destruction of the soul of man and they make one distant from Almighty God, the consequences of which would become clear in the hereafter.

Amirul Momineen (a) said to his son: Allah, the Mighty and Sublime has made good morals as means of connection between Himself and His servants; do you not like to observe morals, which would be means of getting connected to God?[32]

Imam Ja'far Sadiq (a) said: Good morals are ornaments in the world and promenade for the hereafter. Faith of man is perfected through

---

[27] Mustadrakul Wasail, Vol. 8, Pg. 447
[28] Biharul Anwar, Vol. 71, Pg. 389
[29] Biharul Anwar, Vol. 71, Pg. 396
[30] Al-Kafi, Vol. 2, Pg. 100
[31] Al-Kafi, Vol. 2, Pg. 321
[32] Mustadrakul Wasail, Vol. 11, Pg. 192

good morals and it is the means of proximity to God.[33]

The Messenger of Allah (s) said: The things most instrumental to get my followers admitted to Paradise are fear of God and good morals.[34]

Imam Ja'far Sadiq (a) said: Good morals destroys sins just as sun melts ice.[35]

The self of man is a noble essence, which is illuminated, ethereal and is superior to matter, which due to being ethereal is superior to all animals.

It is here that the status of moral values would become clear. Perfection of morals with the humanity of man and its ethereal spirit is having proportion and originality. If we take away perfections and excellence of morals from man, there would be no difference between him and animals.

That is why Islam has emphasized that man should guard his ethereal soul and personal nobility and should always endeavor to strengthen it.

Amirul Momineen (a) said: One who considers his self as great; it would be easy for him to abandon has animal desires.[36]

He also said: One, who considers his self noble, does not besmear it with sins.[37]

He again said: One who is attentive to the nobility of his self; he keeps it from degrading desires.[38]

And he said: Self is a valuable gem, one who takes care of it, scales a lofty position and one who drags it to meanness, has taken it to

---

[33] Mustadrakul Wasail, Vol. 8, Pg. 449

[34] Al-Kafi, Vol. 2, Pg. 100

[35] Al-Kafi, Vol. 2, Pg. 100

[36] Nahjul Balagha, Saying no. 449

[37] Ghurarul Hikam, Pg. 627

[38] Ghurarul Hikam, Pg. 434

lowliness.[39]

In the same way, he said: A noble self will increase compassions.[40]

It is said with regard to perfection of ethics: All human beings in all periods of time and in all the places have consensus on beauty and value. Yes, the pure nature of man possesses such perception and ethical discrimination and the 'should be' and 'should not be' also show this holy perception. It is this same self knowledge and attention to humanity of man that gives control to his ethereal soul over body so that he may control his animal desires and inclinations and may come to the level of gaining human values.

Prophets were also sent to help human beings in this holy struggle, in the path of purification and to strengthen the discipline of self. Prophets say to the people: Why are human beings and not animals. Do not forget your humanity and do not submit to animal desires that you suffer loss. The worst loss is that human being should sink into the terrifying whirlpool of animal desires and lose his humanity and finally enter the world of the hereafter in form of a wild beast.

The Holy Quran says:

"Say: The losers surely are those who shall have lost themselves and their families on the day of resurrection; now surely that is the clear loss.' (39:15)

Amirul Momineen (a) said: I am astonished at one who in the world is in pursuit of his lost property, whereas he has lost his self, but is not in pursuit of it.[41]

---

[39] Ghurarul Hikam, Pg. 227

[40] Ghurarul Hikam, Pg. 600

[41] Ghurarul Hikam, Pg. 460

Ethical Practices

Ethical Practices

In moral science, topics like the following are discussed: Good and evil behavior of man, pleasing and hateful qualities, good and bad deeds, good and bad behavior... to propagate ethical matters, scholars of ethics have used the following practices:

1- Practice of the Prophets

The Prophet of Islam and other divine prophets, in calling people to ethics used encouragement and kind motivation, because their aim was control of selves and to prepare them for actions. Therefore they considered the practice of encouragement as effective.

Ethical topics and problems in the Holy Quran and sayings of the Holy Prophet (s) are mentioned in a scattered way in different contexts and members of audience are also encouraged in different ways.

The practice of Infallible Imams (a) in inviting to ethics was of this same type; that is they have mentioned different ethical topics and problems in widespread and repetitive manner.

2- Academic Practice

Some intellectuals have investigated and compiled ethical topics and problems in a scientific manner. The topic of discussion in the science of ethics is good and bad behavior of man, which affects his success or misfortune in the life of the world and hereafter. In the science of ethics, living a better lifestyle is introduced to man.

Science of ethics is having special topics, whose branches and different problems studied in a proper arranged manner, and its good or bad effect is explained.

Implications of bad ethics are also studied and the bad effects and consequence of each of them is hinted. Ways of avoiding them and purification of the self is also placed in charge of those who are interested. Although to prove a point, rational argument and textual evidences, and sometimes even gnostic and skilled means are employed.

Science of ethics is among the ancient instances of contributions of scholars and philosophers. Socrates, Plato (born 427 B.C.) and Aristotle (born 384 B.C.) were the first Greek philosophers that founded ethics in the form of a science and a part of wisdom (practical wisdom) perfected through other philosophers of Greece.

Western intellectuals and philosophers also, by the contribution of Greek philosophers, have continued discussion of ethics. Books have been written regarding this and schools have come into existence. This has gathered momentum in the past century.

Since morals were a part of the principles of Prophet Musa and Isa (a), Christian and Jew intellectuals are more attentive with regard to sources of morals. By the contribution of Greek philosophy and texts of their own religion the started discussions and research into the topic of ethics and compiled books on them.

In Islam also, in continuation of ethical propagation of the Holy Prophet in this subject two important acts took place:

A: Collection of verses and traditions regarding ethics and their arrangement and interpretation.

B: Giving ethical discussions an academic form.

During the period of the Holy Imams (a), companions of the Prophet started to compile verses and traditions regarding ethics; for example, it is mentioned in the account of Muhammad bin Hasan (born 258 A.H.), a companion of Imam Musa Ibne Ja'far (a): He wrote a book entitled Al-Sunan wal Adaab wa Makarimul Akhlaq.[42] Muhammad bin Sulaiman bin Hasan bin Jaham (237-301 A.H.) also has a book to his

---

[42] Majmaur Rijal, Vol. 5, Pg. 188

credit entitled Al Adaab wal Mawaiz.[43] Such types of titles can be found in the list of writings of some narrators of traditions. Regrettably the mentioned books are lost and we don't know how they were written, but most probably it was classification of traditions about morals.

The first and most comprehensive book, which has compiled and arranged traditions and which has survived to this day, is Al-Kafi. This book was written by Muhammad bin Yaqub Kulaini (died 328 A.H.) and it took him twenty years to complete. The Late Kulaini lived during the period of the Minor Occultation (Ghaibat Sughra) and also met the special deputies of Imam Zamana (a) (Nawwab Khas). This book is one of the most reliable and self sufficient sources of Islamic sciences, which in an extremely beautiful style, has classified different Shia traditions and one of its sections deals especially with traditions of ethics.

Afterwards, other books were also compiled on the same style on the topic of ethics like Sawabul Aamaal wa Iqaabul Aamaal by Late Shaykh Saduq (died 381 A.H.) etc.

In recent times most comprehensive and detailed books have been compiled like: Biharul Anwar, Miratul Uqool dar Sharh Kafi,[44] Wasailush Shia,[45] Mustadrakul Wasail,[46] Wafi[47] and Jami Ahadith Shia, which was written on the directions and under supervision of Ayatullah Sayyid Muhammad Husain Tabatabai Burujardi (1292-1380).

The above books are some collections of traditional reports in which all types of traditions are collected.

In the second part, that is compilation of science of ethics also many

---

[43] Majmaur Rijal, Vol. 5, Pg. 219

[44] Writings of Allamah Majlisi

[45] Writings of Shaykh Hurre Amili

[46] Writings of Haji Noori

[47] Writings of Faiz Kashani

efforts are made. Perhaps the first book in this regard is Tahdhibul Akhlaq wa Tatheerul Araaq written by Ahmad bin Muhammad bin Yaqub Miskuya (died 421 A.H.). He has based and compiled Islamic ethics as a science through the verses of Quran, traditions of infallibles and ethical beliefs of Greek philosophers, like Plato and Aristotle.

After him Khwaja Nasiruddin Tusi (597-672 A.H.) wrote Akhlaq Nasiri and Akhlaq Mohtashimi according to the above sources.

Muhammad Ghazzali (450 A.H. to 505 A.H.) is also from the scholars of moral science. He has also on the basis of verses of Quran, traditions of the Prophet, wise sayings of philosophers and Islamic common parlance wrote Ahyaul Uloom in Arabic and Kimiya Saadat in Persian. Ahyaul Uloom is one of the valuable books of ethics, but regrettably it contains some weak points; that is why Mulla Mohsin Faiz Kashani (1007-1091 A.H.) took up the task of its correction and completion and in this way compiled the book entitled Muhajjatul Baidha fee Ahyaul Ahya, which is a very valuable work.

Muhammad Mahdi Naraqi (died 1209 A.H.) also wrote an important book, Jamius Saadaat. Other books as well are written on the subject of ethics, but we must admit that regretfully as much work as is needed has not been done. In spite of the emphasis that Islam lays on ethics, it expects Muslim scholars that in step with progress of science and changes that have come in the individual and social life of man and appearance of different schools of ethics, they should endeavor to widen the scope and systemize the science of Islamic ethics and should be more earnest in this regard.

Philosophy of Morals

Philosophy of morals is almost a new science. In Philosophy of morals, implications of good and bad ethics of man are not discussed; on the contrary it is a process of moral judgments about good and bad matters, righteousness and evil, merits and demerits and beauty and ugliness. For example whether goodness is a factual quality and has external implication or it is a supposed matter? Whether moral judgments are indicative or creative? How and from where have the ethical 'should be' and 'should not be' been derived? How is it possible to derive a creative result from an indicative situation? What is the meaning of felicity and wickedness? Do they really exist or it is just notional? And…so on.

Philosophy of morals in western countries and academic institutions of the world is the customary and living science. Numerous intellectuals have specialized in this science and have written hundreds of books on this topic and schools have come into existence in this sphere. But regrettably among Muslim intellectuals, it is not having any attraction; neither have we had many specialists in this field nor have contemporary books been written on this subject.

Here, we cannot discuss knowledge and philosophy of morals and research and criticize different moral schools and explain the view of Islam on this subject, but for the introduction of readers, it is necessary to present brief discussions in this regard:

Ethics in the view of Islam

Of the different schools of ethics that have appeared, most display a broad minded world view and thinking of the followers of those schools; school of Islamic ethics is also a consequence of its particular world view.

In Islamic world view, there is existence of a divine being; who has created them and is controlling them. Man is a being that everlasting and ever living; that is not destroyed by death, on the contrary, he is transferred from this world to the abode of the hereafter so that he may receive the rewards of his good deeds and be punished for his evil acts.

It considers man to be a being, who is responsible and having a free will; who is not created without an aim, on the contrary he is created for gaining of human perfection and rising up towards Almighty Allah and finally for a beautiful, happy and illuminated life of the hereafter. Man is a being having two dimensions:

On one side he is a beast having animal desires and physical needs, which are related to animal life and which have to be fulfilled in any way.

On the other side he is having an ethereal soul, having superiority over other animals. That is why he became the vicegerent of Allah and gained precedence on angels. The spiritual and internal life of man is also having felicity or wretchedness; in case man reached his aimed perfection in such a way that he develops his ethereal and human aspects and moderates animal desires to the limit of need.

It is at this point that the position of ethical values becomes clear; the same spiritual perfections, which are related to the ethereal soul of man and which have compatibility and which illuminate and comfort the soul of man.

However, bad morals and being immersed in animal lusts, is contrary to the ethereal soul and noble essence of man and weakens, degrades and lowers the aspects of humanity.

Although Islam considers moral values to be compatible to the pure nature of man, but does not consider this much sufficient in enjoining good morals and refraining from bad behavior and does not accept natural morals and non-religious morals, therefore in order to develop faith in God and resurrection and glad tidings of the hereafter and threats of the chastisements of Hell, it calls people to good morals and behavior.

Morals in Islam are based on faith in God and resurrection and hope for rewards of the hereafter and fear of punishment, which are the best guarantees of it effectiveness. As a result of faith in God and gaining His satisfaction, one can in a better way dominate selfishness and animal desires and it revives human values like loyalty, sacrifice, defense of oppressed, confrontation with tyranny, seeking justice, Jihad, trustworthiness, honesty and doing a good turn to others.

In Islam basically the value of every act depends on faith and intention of divine proximity. So much so that moral values lead to perfection and rectitude of man only if they are accompanied with faith and intention of divine proximity and if not, they have no real value; even though they might be regarded as values in public opinion.

Types of ethical problems

Ethical topics and problems can be divided into two groups:

First group: Individual ethics like: attention to God, love for God, reliance on God, being satisfied with the satisfaction of God, sincerity, hopefulness, patience, spiritual needlessness, valor, steadfastness, self contentment, absoluteness in act etc., which are good qualities.

In the same way, show off, self conceit, jealousy, anger, anxiety, despair, haste and impatience, materialism and love of position, fear, greed, feeling insecurity, faithlessness, not being satisfied with God's will, indetermination etc., which are from the bad moral traits.

Second group: Social ethics like truthfulness, nice behavior, humility, respect for others, well wishing, doing good to others, trustworthiness, forgiveness, goodness to parents, good relations with relatives, fulfilling the rights of others, arranging the affairs of Muslims, cognition of duties etc., which are from the manners of life and social good morals.

In the same way, bad nature and behavior, arrogance, disrespect for others, insulting people, betraying trust, lying, breaking of oath, exposing the secrets of others, ill behavior with others, non-fulfillment of the rights of others, carelessness of the matters of Muslims, creating mischief, helping the oppressors, wasteful expenditure and miserliness, which are from the social evil morals.

These and similar points are mentioned in Quran and books of ethics and are explained and expounded therein. Those who are interested can refer to them.

Supplication (Dua)

Supplication (Dua)

The dictionary meaning of Dua is to request someone for something. Dua is fulfilled when the one who is addressed is intelligent and aware and has the capability to fulfill that request. On the basis of this, plants and animals are never asked for anything. In the same way, no request is made to the helpless man, except those whom they consider as having power. A servant who raises his hands to Almighty Allah to supplicate, it is so because he considers Him as present, witnessing, kind, needless and absolutely powerful.

To supplicate is a natural need for man, because he is needful and whatever he has is from Almighty Allah and without His bestowals, he does not survive even for a moment. He is connected to God in his being, qualities and acts. In solving his problems and fulfillment of his needs, this weak being is having no choice, except to stretch hands of needs to the needless Lord and to request Him for the same. Dua is among the signs of servitude; it is a cure for internal pains and it gives hope to man. If man during hardships, had no satisfactory refuge, how he could have continued his life? If in removing problems, he does not seek the refuge of powerful and kind God, whose refuge he would seek?

Dua is one of the best worship acts, because worship is in the meaning of extreme humility and expression of servitude and this same meaning is actualized in Dua. In Quran and traditions also, Dua is considered as a worship act; the Holy Quran says:

"And your Lord says: Call upon Me, I will answer you; surely those who are too proud for My service shall soon enter hell abased." (40:60)

In this verse, omission of Dua is considered arrogance and selfishness.

Hannan bin Sudair has narrated from his father that he said: I asked Imam Muhammad Baqir (a): Which are the best worship deeds? He replied: Nothing is better in the view of Allah than that He should be begged from and nothing is more hateful than that arrogance should be shown in His worship and that nothing is asked from Him.[48]

Saif says: I heard Imam Ja'far Sadiq (a) say: Supplicate, because nothing takes you closer to Almighty Allah as Dua. In secondary matters also, take the refuge of God, because the minor matters are in the hand of one who has major affairs under His control.[49]

Hammad says: I heard Imam Ja'far Sadiq (a) say: Supplicate and don't say that everything is over; because Dua is a worship act. Almighty Allah says in the Holy Quran: surely those who are too proud for My service shall soon enter hell abased. And He says: Call upon Me, I will answer you.[50]

On the basis of this, Dua is a worship act, which is performed with intention of seeking proximity to Almighty Allah and it brings the person close to Him and also makes him eligible for heavenly rewards. A servant must, at all times, and on all occasions, keep his hands stretched before the powerful and kind Lord and seek his needs from Him. Dua can be made in any words and in any language; but the best are supplications that we have received from the Holy Prophet (s) and the Holy Imams (a), because they are more cognizant than us about our true needs.

Question: Since Almighty Allah has promised fulfillment of Dua, why in so many instances supplication is not answered?

The Holy Quran says:

---

[48] Al-Kafi, Vol. 2, Pg. 486

[49] Al-Kafi, Vol. 2, Pg. 467

[50] Al-Kafi, Vol. 2, Pg. 467

> *"And when My servants ask you concerning Me, then surely I am very near; I answer the prayer of the suppliant when he calls on Me, so they should answer My call and believe in Me that they may walk in the right way." (2:186)*

Answer: Almighty Allah in this same verse has made acceptance of Dua conditional by the phrase of 'when he calls on Me'; that is he should call only Me; and this is a very important point. It can be concluded from the verse that Dua is answered only when a person calls Almighty Allah with a sincere heart and does not pay attention to anyone or anything other than Him. Thus aloofness from anyone or anything other than God and stretching ones hands to God is one of the conditions of acceptance of Dua. Whenever this condition is fulfilled, it would be accepted. But most supplications are not as such; on the contrary they are issued in form of texts, which are accompanied by mental notions, but the inner part of the being are related more to natural causes and reasons and since true supplications are not recited, they are not accepted.

The same point can be concluded from some traditions:

Sulaiman bin Umar says: I heard Imam Ja'far Sadiq (a) say: Allah the Mighty and Sublime does not fulfill the supplication of a person who supplicates without attention and without presence of mind. When you address the Almighty Allah, you should make your heart attentive to Him and you should have certainty that it'd be fulfilled.[51]

Amirul Momineen (a) said: Allah, the Mighty and Sublime does not accept the supplication, which is recited in an absent minded manner.[52]

---

[51] Al-Kafi, Vol. 2, Pg. 473

[52] Al-Kafi, Vol. 2, Pg. 473

Imam Musa Ibne Ja'far (a) said: Some companions of Imam Ja'far Sadiq (a) said to him: How is that when we supplicate, our supplications are not answered? He replied: Because you call one whom you don't recognize.[53]

Imam Musa Ibne Ja'far (a) has narrated from his father, Imam Ja'far bin Muhammad (a) and he has narrated from his ancestors from the Messenger of Allah (s) that he said: Allah says: I cut off the paths to the heavens and the earth for one who seeks the mediation of creatures, except Me; thus if he asks Me, I don't give and if he calls Me, I don't reply. Every servant who focuses his attention on Me and not to My servants, heavens and earth guarantee his sustenance. Thus if they call Me, I reply and if he asks me, I give and if he seeks My forgiveness, I forgive him.[54]

Also, sometimes the reason for non-acceptance of supplication is that Almighty Allah does not regard it to be in the interest of man if his Dua is answered. Therefore He gives precedence to his interests over that of accepting his Dua. It is known that every intelligent human being is in fact desirous of his well being; in such way that if he knew that it is not in his interest, he would never request it from Almighty Allah. It is in this instance that Almighty Allah does not fulfill his recited supplication.

Sometimes the Almighty Allah, who is kind and merciful, gives precedence to the well being of man in the hereafter over that of the fulfillment of his worldly prayers. He does not respond to the supplication of one He loves too much, so that he may always continue to beseech Him and whisper to Him in secret and through this may become eligible for lofty rewards in the hereafter.

---

[53] Biharul Anwar, Vol. 93, Pg. 368
[54] Biharul Anwar, Vol. 71, Pg. 155

The same point is mentioned in traditions:

Ishaq bin Ammar has narrated from Imam Ja'far Sadiq (a) that he said: A believer servant supplicates Almighty Allah for something; thus Allah, the Mighty and Sublime says: I delay the acceptance of the Dua of My servant, because I like to hear his voice and his supplication. On Judgment Day, Almighty Allah says: My servant, You called Me, but I delayed the acceptance of your prayer and your reward is such and such. You also supplicated me for so and so thing and I delayed its acceptance, and your reward is such and such. At that moment, the believer servant wishes that alas if none of his supplications were accepted so that he would have been rewarded with a better reward in the hereafter.[55]

On the basis of this, no supplication is without effect and people should not be careless of this important worship act.

Question: It is possible that someone might say that Dua is useless, because that which a person asks from Allah or that which is divinely ordained whose natural cause has appeared in such a way that it would occur without Dua, or that it is not a part of divine will and its natural cause has not appeared, in this case Dua will also not be effective in its fulfillment, because Allah, the Mighty and the High brings everything into existence through natural causes: Allah has left the matters to take their natural course.

Answer: Islam also does not deny the effect of natural causes, but in case of Dua it can be said that it becomes a part cause of the thing and by its accomplishment, the perfect cause is accomplished and the effect comes into being. On the basis of this, the desire of the supplicant in the instance that it is accepted will not be fulfilled without existence of its complete cause; on the contrary, it would be fulfilled following the completion of cause as Dua is also a part of it. But if Dua is not

---

[55] Al-Kafi, Vol. 2, Pg. 490

fulfilled, such cause would also not appear, on the basis of this, it is possible to change destiny through Dua.

Imam Ja'far Sadiq (a) said: Dua cancels divine decree that descends from the heavens and which has been confirmed.[56]

Umar bin Yazid says: I heard Imam Musa Ibne Ja'far (a) say: Dua cancels that which is ordained or not ordained. The narrators asked: I understand that which is ordained; but what is the meaning of that which is not ordained? He replied: Till the time it comes into existence.[57]

Abdullah bin Sinan says: I heard Imam Ja'far Sadiq (a) say: Dua cancels the destiny, which has been decided, Supplicate more, because Dua is key to mercy and a channel of fulfillment of one desires. You cannot reach that which is with Almighty Allah without Dua. It is hoped that the door, which is knocked too much would be opened at last.[58]

Abu Wallad has narrated that Imam Musa Ibne Ja'far (a) said: It is necessary for you to supplicate, because Dua is for Almighty Allah and to ask from Him. Dua wards off calamities that are ordained and decreed; and which do not remain, except with the authority of God. Thus when Allah, the Mighty and Sublime is called, He withdraws the calamity.[59]

Worship in Islam

Worship in Islam

---

[56] Al-Kafi, Vol. 2, Pg. 469
[57] Al-Kafi, Vol. 2, Pg. 469
[58] Al-Kafi, Vol. 2, Pg. 470
[59] Al-Kafi, Vol. 2, Pg. 470

The dictionary meaning of worship is submission, obedience and expression of humility. Raghib says: Servitude is in the meaning of humility, but worship is higher than that; because it is in the meaning of extreme expression of humility. From this aspect, no one other than Allah is worthy of worship.[60]

The word of 'servant' (a'bd) is also derived from the same root and it is in the meaning of a slave. Slaves are those who submit to the authority of the master and the latter has the right to intervene in all their affairs.

On the basis of this, every human being can be called as a slave and a servant, because they are all subjects of Allah. But the ownership of Allah, the Mighty and the High with regard to people as compared to the ownership of people with regard to slaves is having a fundamental difference, because the ownership of human beings is suppositional, but the ownership of Allah, the Mighty and Sublime is real and original. Beings depend on God for their existence and survival and are at His discretion and disposal. Poverty and needfulness is a part of their being and none of it belongs to God.

> *"O men! you are they who stand in need of Allah, and Allah is He Who is the Self-sufficient, the Praised One." (35:15)*

From this it became clear that all human beings and existing beings of the world are truly servants and subjects of Almighty Allah, because they submit to the laws of the ruler over the world and will of the powerful God and they cannot oppose it.

The Holy Quran says:

---

[60] Al-Mufradat, Pg. 319

> *"There is no one in the heavens and the earth but will come to the Beneficent God as a servant." (19:93)*

That which was mentioned was in the literal meaning of worship and natural worship. But worship in legal terminology is: Expression of servitude and extreme humility and submission before divine commands; it consists of some special rituals, which are called worship acts. His followers perform those acts as an expression of servitude and seek the proximity of their deity.

In Islam also, such rituals are legislated, like prayers, fast and Hajj.

All the beings of the world are in need of Almighty Allah and except for Almighty Allah no one can fulfill those needs. On the basis of this, except for Allah no one is able to become a deity. Man is duty bound to worship Allah alone.

Prophets called human beings to the worship of one God and warned them against worship of anything or anyone other than Him.

The Messenger of Allah also called people to belief in the unity of Godhead and to negate polytheism. He prohibited them from the worship of anything or anyone other than Him and this was the greatest aim of His Eminence.

Quran is also a book of monotheism and it calls people to the worship of One God:

> *"(This is) a Book, whose verses are made decisive, then are they made plain, from the Wise, All-aware: That you shall not serve (any) but Allah; surely I am a warner for you from Him and a giver of good news." (11:1-2)*

On the basis of this, every act, which is performed with intention of worship, divine rewards and proximity, should be only for Almighty

Allah; otherwise it would be counted as polytheism.

One of the conditions of acceptance of worship is sincerity and intention of proximity.

On the basis of this, if one performs a worship act for show off, his act is invalid and not only would it not earn rewards, it also debases the soul of man and makes him eligible for divine chastisement. That is why show off has been condemned and is considered to be a type of polytheism. Imam Ja'far Sadiq (a) said:

Every kind of show off is polytheism, one who does something to show off to people should take its rewards from the people and one who performs an act for Almighty Allah, He gives it reward.[61]

Ali bin Saalim says: I heard Imam Ja'far Sadiq (a) say: Allah, the Mighty and Sublime says: I am the best partner; one who makes someone other than Me as a partner in his act, I don't accept that deed.[62]

On the basis of this, man should make efforts to make his worship sincere and solely for the sake of Almighty Allah and His proximity and he should at ant cost avoid show off and flamboyance. As much a deed is sincere as much divine reward is there for it.

However, it should be only through rituals of worship and devotions commanded by Allah, and specified by the Prophet and the Holy Imams (a) and not anyone else. No one has the right to invent a worship act on his own, without supporting reliable legal evidence. Evidences of worship acts, whether obligatory or recommended require reliable legal proof. Acts, which are ordered to be performed in Quran and authentic and correct traditions, can be performed as worship acts with intention of proximity. Muslims must be obedient to laws of Shariah.

---

[61] Al-Kafi, Vol. 2, Pg. 293

[62] Al-Kafi, Vol. 2, Pg. 295

Innovation in religion is one of the divinely prohibited acts and it is obligatory on scholars of religion to confront it.

Imam Ja'far Sadiq (a) has narrated that the Messenger of Allah (s) said: Innovation is deviation and deviation is the cause of entry into Hell.[63]

Yunus bin Abdur Rahman says: I asked Imam Musa bin Ja'far (a): How can I become a monotheist? He replied: O Yunus do not be an innovator in religion. One, who acts according to his personal opinion, is destroyed. One, who abandons the Ahle Bayt of the Prophet, becomes misguided and one who deserts the Quran and sayings of the Prophet, becomes a disbeliever.[64]

Zurarah says: I asked Imam Ja'far Sadiq (a) about the lawful and the prohibited in Islam. He replied: The lawful of Muhammad would remain lawful till Judgment Day and his unlawful would be unlawful till Judgment Day. There is nothing else and neither would it come into being. He also said: Imam Ali (a) said: No one creates an innovation in religion, except one who leaves a practice of the Prophet.[65]

The Messenger of Allah (s) said: When an innovation appears in my Ummah it is obligatory for the scholar to express his knowledge and to confront that heresy. If he does not do this, the curse of Allah would be on him.[66]

Worship in Islam is of two kinds: Obligatory and recommended: Obligatory worship acts are deeds, which the legislator of the holy religion of Islam (Allah) has made obligatory on human beings to be performed with intention of proximity and in the right manner and if he leaves them without a valid excuse, he would be liable for punishment in the hereafter like in case of obligatory prayers,

---

[63] Al-Kafi, Vol. 1, Pg. 57
[64] Al-Kafi, Vol. 1, Pg. 56
[65] Al-Kafi, Vol. 1, Pg. 58
[66] Al-Kafi, Vol. 1, Pg. 54

obligatory fasts and obligatory Hajj, etc.

Recommended worship acts are deeds, which the duty bound are supposed to perform with intention of proximity. If they perform them, they would be rewarded for it, but if they leave it, they would not become eligible for any punishment; like recommended prayers, Ziyarats, recitation of Quran, supplications etc. However, except in case of existence of reliable legal proof, its validity and reward is dependant on intention of proximity and any kind of show off invalidates it.

Part III: Islam and Faith

Islam

Islam

The literary meaning of Islam is obedience and submission and terminologically it means acceptance of the religion of Islam. Prophet Muhammad (s) propagated the religion of Islam and his followers are called as Muslims, because they have surrendered themselves to Allah and His heavenly laws.

The Holy Quran says:

> "And who has a better religion than he who submits himself entirely to Allah? And he is the doer of good (to others) and follows the faith of Ibrahim, the upright one, and Allah took Ibrahim as a friend." (4:125)

In Quran, it is clearly mentioned that the religion of Ibrahim (a) was also in the meaning of Islam. He was a Muslim and requested Allah for his descendants and community to be Muslim. In the same way, it is mentioned in Quran:

"Ibrahim was not a Jew or a Christian but he was (an) upright (man), a Muslim, and he was not one of the polytheists." (3:67)

And He says:

"Our Lord, and make us both submissive to Thee and (raise) from our offspring a nation submitting to Thee, and show us our ways of devotion and turn to us (mercifully), surely Thou art the Oft-returning (to mercy), the Merciful." (2:128)

In the same way, He says:

"And strive hard in (the way of) Allah, (such) a striving as is due to Him; He has chosen you and has not laid upon you any hardship in religion; the faith of your father Ibrahim; He named you Muslims before..." (22:78)

And also, He says:

"Surely the (true) religion with Allah is Islam, and those to whom the Book had been given did not show opposition, but after knowledge had come to them, out of envy among themselves; and whoever disbelieves in the communications

of Allah then surely Allah is quick in reckoning." (3:19)

In another place, He says:

"And whoever desires a religion other than Islam, it shall not be accepted from him, and in the hereafter he shall be one of the losers." (3:85)

One who confesses to the three fundamentals would be considered a Muslim: Monotheism, resurrection and prophethood of Prophet Muhammad (s). Acceptance of these three fundamentals makes him eligible for legacies of Islam like purification, justification of marriage with Muslims, inheritance and security of life and property.

Qasim Sairafi says: Imam Ja'far Sadiq (a) said: By Islam, life of man remains sacred and secure, his trusts are restored and marriage becomes lawful with him, but the (divine) reward depends on faith.[67]

However, every Islam does not become eligible for success in the hereafter; on the contrary these effects are only related to the Islam, which springs from the inner conscience of man and which is accompanied with acting on the religious duties. From this aspect in traditions performance of obligatory acts is introduced as a pillar of Islam. Abu Hamza has narrated from Imam Muhammad Baqir (a) that he said: Islam is based on five pillars: Prayer, Zakat, Fast, Hajj and Wilayat. However nothing is emphasized as much as Wilayat.[68]

---

[67] Al-Kafi, Vol. 2, Pg. 24
[68] Al-Kafi, Vol. 2, Pg. 18

Faith

Faith

The literary meaning of Faith is confidence, peace of mind and absence of doubt and terminologically it means tranquility in the existence of the creator of the world and His oneness and certainty in the existence of resurrection and life after death and sincere testimony (acceptance) of prophethood of the Prophet of Islam.

Raghib has written in this regard: Faith means acceptance of truth and testifying to it and this matter is fulfilled when three factors come together: confession by the heart, acceptance by tongue and acting according to that.[69]

The root of Faith is the same belief and confidence of the mind, but fulfillment of religious duties is its necessary requirement. It is not possible for a person to have faith in something and to act in opposition to that. If his act is not in accordance to his claim, his Faith is not true.

The Holy Quran says:

> *"You shall not find a people who believe in Allah and the latter day befriending those who act in opposition to Allah and His Apostle, even though they were their (own) fathers, or their sons, or their brothers, or their kinsfolk; these are they into whose hearts He has impressed faith, and whom He has strengthened with an inspiration from Him: and He will cause them to enter gardens beneath which rivers flow, abiding therein; Allah is well-pleased with them and they are well-pleased with Him; these are Allah's party: now*

---

[69] Al-Mufradat, Pg. 26

surely the party of Allah are the successful ones." (58:22)

Muhammad bin Muslim says: I asked Imam Ja'far Sadiq (a) about Faith and he said: Testifying to the oneness of God, and that Muhammad is the Messenger of Allah and that which he has brought is from Almighty Allah. Testimony to these matters from the depth of the heart constitutes faith. Muhammad bin Muslim asked: Is testimony not itself an act? He replied: Yes, there can be no faith without deeds. Deed is a part of faith. Without that faith is not proved.[70]

Three conditions are necessary for Faith:

1. Sincere confidence in the oneness of Allah, certainty on resurrection and life after death and confession to the rightfulness of the prophethood of the Prophet of Islam.

2. Verbal testimony of these same points:

3. Performance of the duties of religion, which is the necessary condition for faith and sincere certainty.

On the basis of this, Faith is superior to Islam, because Islam can be fulfilled by testimony to three points even if sincere certainty is not there. But in faith, in addition to verbal testimony, certainty and sincere confidence is also required. Thus, every believer is a Muslim, but every Muslim is not a believer.

Sama'a says: I asked Imam Ja'far Sadiq (a): Is there a difference between faith and Islam? He replied: Faith includes Islam, but Islam does not include faith. I asked: Then describe faith and Islam. He replied:

Islam means testifying to the oneness of God and prophethood of the Prophet of Islam. With these testimonies, a person becomes a Muslim, his life becomes secure and it makes him eligible to marry and inherit. Islam of Muslims is according to this outward form.

---

[70] Al-Kafi, Vol. 2, Pg. 38

But faith is guidance, sincere certainty and action according to that. Faith is a rank above Islam; although it is included in Islam, its apparent form, but in it is not so in its inner part.[71]

Almighty Allah says in the Holy Quran:

> *"The dwellers of the desert say: We believe. Say: You do not believe but say, We submit; and faith has not yet entered into your hearts..." (49:14)*

Jamil bin Darraj says: I asked Imam Ja'far Sadiq (a) about the interpretation of the verse: "The dwellers of the desert say: We believe. Say: You do not believe but say, We submit; and faith has not yet entered into your hearts..." (49:14) He said: Do you not know that faith is other than Islam?[72]

Humran bin Ayyin has narrated that Imam Muhammad Baqir (a) said: Faith is something, which enters the heart and which propels him to God. Obedience and submission to the commands of Almighty Allah also testify true faith. But Islam is the same apparent word and deed and it is the same, which people follow. This Islam becomes makes ones life secure and is a justification for marriage and inheritance.

Muslims have consensus on prayer, Zakat, Fast and Hajj and in this way they have come out of disbelief and have been related to faith. Faith is not included in Islam, but Islam is common with faith. Faith and Islam have come together in words and deeds just as Kaaba is inside Masjidul Haraam, but the Masjid is not inside the Kaaba. In the same way, Islam is included in faith, but faith is not included with it.

---

[71] Al-Kafi, Vol. 2, Pg. 25

[72] Al-Kafi, Vol. 2, Pg. 24

Almighty Allah says in Quran:

> *"The dwellers of the desert say: We believe. Say: You do not believe but say, We submit; and faith has not yet entered into your hearts..." (49:14)*[73]

Thus the statement of Almighty Allah is the truest of all.

However, it must be said that faith is having ranks and stages. All believers are not in the same stage from the aspect of confidence of the heart; on the contrary they have different ranks, because faith of individuals is capable of perfection and development.

Almighty Allah says:

> *"Those only are believers whose hearts become full of fear when Allah is mentioned, and when His communications are recited to them they increase them in faith, and in their Lord do they trust." (8:2)*

Abdul Aziz says: Imam Ja'far Sadiq (a) said to me: O Abdul Aziz, faith is having ten stages: like one climbs a ladder taking one step after another. Thus one who stands at the second rung should not tell the one who is on the first that you are worthless in the same you must not humiliate those who stand below your level, otherwise the one who is above you would degrade you. When you find someone below your level, you must try to bring him upto your level in a congenial manner and do not make him carry that which he cannot lift; for in that case his faith would be ruined and one who ruins the faith of a believer is supposed

---

[73] Al-Kafi, Vol. 2, Pg. 26

to make amends for it.[74]

Allamah Majlisi (r.a.) writes in this regard: The fact is that faith is susceptible to increase and decrease, because we consider deeds to be a part of faith, or its condition or its effect, because as much strong the faith is, its effects are more on the limbs and physical parts. Thus, increase or decrease of deeds proves the intensity or weakness of faith. Every stage of faith is followed by its appropriate deeds; when the believer performs that deed, his faith also becomes stronger.

On the other hand, when the believer commits a greater sin, his faith is harmed to the limit that it is possible for him to lose the essence of faith. One, who has faith in Allah and resurrection; how is it possible for him to commit a sin, which would make him liable to be sent to Hell? Thus, committing of sins is not, but due to the weakness of certainty.[75]

Disbelief

Disbelief

Disbelief, in the literary meaning is 'to hide' or 'to conceal' and in terminology it is the opposite of Islam. Every non-Muslim is considered as a disbeliever. As we mentioned, there are three conditions in fulfillment of Islam: (1) Testimony to the oneness of God, (2) Belief in resurrection and life after death and (3) Testifying to the messengership

---

[74] Al-Kafi, Vol. 2, Pg. 45

[75] Biharul Anwar, Vol. 69, Pg. 210

of Prophet Muhammad (s). But if one denies any or all of these principles, he is a disbeliever and the conditions of Islam will not be applicable to him.

Almighty Allah says in the Holy Quran:

> *"And whoever does not believe in Allah and His Apostle, then surely We have prepared burning fire for the unbelievers." (48:13)*

And in another chapter, He says:

> *"O you who believe! believe in Allah and His Apostle and the Book, which He has revealed to His Apostle and the Book, which He revealed before; and whoever disbelieves in Allah and His angels and His apostles and the last day, he indeed strays off into a remote error." (4:136)*

And He says:

> *"And those who disbelieve say: You are not a messenger. Say: Allah is sufficient as a witness between me and you and whoever has knowledge of the Book." (13:43)*

In another verse, He says:

> *"And whoever invokes with Allah another god - he has no proof of this - his reckoning is only with his Lord; surely the unbelievers shall not be successful." (23:117)*

On the basis of this, one who is a denier of God or prophethood of the Prophet of Islam or resurrection and life after death is a disbeliever. In the same way, if one has doubt in any or all of these principles, he is a disbeliever.

The Holy Quran says:

> *"And those who disbelieve shall not cease to be in doubt concerning it until the hour overtakes them suddenly, or there comes on them the chastisement of a destructive day."* (22:55)

Imam Ja'far Sadiq (a) said: One who doubts in the existence of God or His Messenger, is a disbeliever.[76]

Amirul Momineen (a) said: Do not fall into uncertainty, lest you fall into doubt and do not fall into doubt, lest you become a disbeliever.[77]

It is can be concluded for above verses and traditions that doubt in one of the principles of religion makes one liable to disbelief even though it might not be accompanied by verbal denial. But it can be concluded from some traditions that doubt that appears to a person in solitude does not make him a disbeliever; on the contrary, it is verbal denial, which makes him a disbeliever.

Muhammad bin Muslim says: I was seated to the left of Imam Ja'far Sadiq (a) and Zurarah was to his right. At that moment Abu Basir entered and asked: O Aba Abdullah, what is your view about one who has doubt in the existence of God? He replied: He is a disbeliever. He

---

[76] Al-Kafi, Vol. 2, Pg. 386

[77] Al-Kafi, Vol. 2, Pg. 399

further asked: What if he has doubt in the prophethood of Prophet Muhammad (s)? He replied: He is a disbeliever. At that moment he turned to Zurarah and said: He becomes a disbeliever in case he denies.[78]

Zurarah has narrated from Imam Ja'far Sadiq (a) that he said: If people reserve their judgment about something they have no knowledge of without denying, they don't become disbelievers.[79]

On the basis of this, if one has doubts in the existence of God or prophethood of Prophet Muhammad (s) or resurrection, but he does not deny in words and his aim is to investigate and not to deny; such a person will not be considered a disbeliever.

Confirmed denier: One of the causes of denial is negation of the fundamental principles of religion. It is said that if one denies one of the necessary principles of religion like the obligation of prayer or paying of Zakat etc., while he knows that the mentioned order is among the necessary commands of religion, he is a disbeliever, because through this act, he denies the oneness of God or the messengership of the Prophet of Islam. Therefore the criterion of denial is negation of one of the principles of faith and one who negates one of the fundamentals of faith is a disbeliever and the rules of disbelief would apply on him. But one, who accepts all these fundamentals and testifies to their correctness, is a Muslim and the rules of Islam are applicable on him.

On the basis of this, Shia and the four schools of Ahle Sunnat (Hanafi, Maliki, Shafei and Hanbali) are Muslims, since they have faith in the principles of religion.

Religious Rulings Apperatined to disbelief

Disbeliever is having special rules in Islam and some of them are as follows:

---

[78] Al-Kafi, Vol. 2, Pg. 339

[79] Al-Kafi, Vol. 2, Pg. 388

1. Muslim men and women cannot marry disbeliever men and women in a permanent marriage;
2. A disbeliever does not inherit from a Muslim.
3. A disbeliever is ritually impure (Najis).

Hypocrisy

Hypocrisy

In the terminology of Quran, a hypocrite is one who is apparently a Muslim and who testifies to the fundamentals of religion, but in fact he is a disbeliever and he does not have faith in what he claims. Such a person is a Muslim and the rules of Islam would be applicable to him. However, such faith is of no use to his success in the hereafter and on Judgment Day he would be punished like the disbelievers; on the contrary more severely than them. The Holy Quran says:

> *"When the hypocrites come to you, they say: We bear witness that you are most surely Allah's Apostle; and Allah knows that you are most surely His Apostle, and Allah bears witness that the hypocrites are surely liars. They make their oaths a shelter, and thus turn away from Allah's way; surely evil is that which they do. That is because they believe, then disbelieve, so a seal is set upon their hearts, so that they do not understand." (63:1-3)*

Appearance of hypocrites

The accurate history of the origin of hypocrites is not known, but it is definite that they were present before as well as after the Hijrat (migration to Medina). Since they had not accepted Islam with certainty, but due to different objectives they claimed to be Muslims and in this way they entered the ranks of Muslims. They consist of the following groups:

First group: Those, who with the aim of getting position and status and to take advantage of supposed power of Islam, admitted themselves in the group of Muslims. Such people existed in Mecca as well as in Medina when Muslims gained power, because in the beginning of the call also, it was not remote that Islam will become popular one day and the Prophet and his companions will emerge victorious on the enemies and gain a formidable power. However, this possibility became stronger in Medina; that is why the number of hypocrites increased.

In such circumstances, there was possibility that hostile persons and opportunists would take advantage and cooperate with minority, although they did not have sincere belief in those principles.

Second group: Those who did not accept Islam with sincerity, but they did so for fear of death and danger to their interests they apparently recited the dual formula of faith verbally. These hypocrites were in Medina as well as after the conquest of Mecca they apparently accepted Islam and entered the Islamic community.

Third group: Those who had really accepted Islam, but later on they apostasied, because of doubts; but in order to survive they concealed their disbelief.

On the basis of this, hypocrites existed among the Muslims throughout the lifetime of the Prophet of Islam (s) and after his passing away some of them remained in the same way in the Muslim society.

Conspiracies of hypocrites

They had concealed their inward disbelief and lived among the Muslims and many a times through their hypocritical actions they posed themselves to be true Muslims and well wishers of Islam and Muslims. In this way they attracted the confidence of Muslims, but inwardly they conspired against them and tried to create mischief for them. Therefore, numerous problems appeared for Muslims, which were not lesser than the plots of infidels and polytheists. Below we mention some of the instances:

A group of hypocrites formed a secret party, who in their secret gatherings ridiculed the Prophet of Islam (s) and criticized the verses of Quran. Sometimes they also mentioned all this in the presence of new converts to Islam. In addition to this, they spread doubts and misgivings in order to weaken the faith of Muslims. On different pretexts, they kept away from taking part in normal Muslim rituals of Friday Prayer, congregations and Jihad and by exaggerating the power of enemies discouraged the Muslims from taking part in fighting. Sometimes they also resorted to flight from the battlefield and at the same time instigated the brave ones to also flee. They extended secret cooperation with the enemies of Islam and conveyed official and confidential information to them.

A group of hypocrites constructed a Masjid near the Quba Masjid and invited the Prophet to establish congregational prayer in it. The Messenger of Allah (s) asked: What is your aim in constructing this Masjid? They said: We have made it for rainy nights and for the ailing persons who cannot attend congregational prayer in your Masjid, and there is no other aim in it.

While the fact was that they had some other aim in it. They had made the Masjid with intention to create dissension, harm Islam and spread disunity among the Muslims. In the same way, they used it as a center to spread conspiracies and plots against Muslims and to support disbelief and polytheism. However Quran exposed their conspiracy and mentioned their true aim; and that is why it labeled it as Masjid Zirar (Masjid of harms).

The Holy Quran says:

> *"And those who built a Masjid to cause harm and for unbelief and to cause disunion among the believers and an ambush to him who made war against Allah and His Apostle before; and they will certainly swear: We did not desire aught but good; and Allah bears witness that they are most surely liars. Never stand in it; certainly a Masjid founded on piety from the very first day is more deserving that you should stand in it; in it are men who love that they should be purified; and Allah loves those who purify themselves."* (9:107-108)

When the Messenger of Allah (s) was informed about the aim of hypocrites, he did not accept their invitation to lead prayers in their Masjid and ordered some of his companions to burn down Masjid Zirar and to raze it to the ground.[80]

One of the breaches of trust of hypocrites, which is also mentioned in the Holy Quran, took place after the battle against Bani Mustaliq; that is when information reached the Prophet of Islam (s) that the Bani Mustaliq tribe has prepared itself to attack the Muslims. The Holy Prophet (s) declared Jihad among the Muslims. Muslim stalwarts prepared themselves and marched towards the land of enemies with the Messenger of Allah (s). They landed at the Marisi well and the battle took place at the same spot. After a brief battle, soldiers of

---

[80] Majmaul Bayan, Vol. 5, Pg. 73

Islam gained domination over enemies from Bani Mustaliq. They slew some of them and took some as captives. After this victory a dispute developed between Muhajireen and Ansar with regard to the water of the Marisi well and it almost developed into a civil war.

Abdullah bin Ubayy, one of the hypocrites of Medina, who nursed extraordinary grudge against Islam and participated in the battles only to share the war booty, expressed his enmity and hypocrisy and spoke thus to those who had gathered around him: "All this is the result of our own doing. We provided quarters to the Muhajireen of Mecca in our land and protected them from their enemies. Our condition conforms to the well-known saying: "Nourish your dog and it will bite you. By Allah, when we return to Medina it will be necessary that the strong and dignified people (of Medina) should turn out the weak ones (i.e. the Muhajireen)."

The speech of Abdullah before the people, in whose minds the Arabian party-spirit and the ideas of the Age of Ignorance still lurked, had a very unwholesome effect on them and it was possible that their unity might have been jeopardized.

Fortunately, however, a zealous Muslim, named Zaid bin Arqam, who was also present there, replied to his satanic words with full force and said: "By Allah, you are the person, who is mean and humble. You are the person, who doesn't enjoy the least position amongst his kinsmen. On the contrary, Prophet Muhammad (s) is respectable amongst the Muslims and their hearts are filled with love for him."

Then he departed from there and came to the Prophet and informed him of the seditious speech of Abdullah. To keep up appearance, the Prophet rejected the words of Zaid thrice and said: "Maybe you are mistaken. Probably anger actuated you to say this. It is possible that he considered you to be low and foolish and meant nothing else." However, Zaid replied in the negative with regard to all these possibilities and said: "No, his intention was to create differences and to fan dissensions."

Abdullah learned about Zaid bin Arqam's conversation with the Prophet. He came before the Prophet immediately and said: "I never said any such words." Some well-wishers of his also supported him and said that Zaid had erred in quoting him. The Holy Prophet (s) wanted to do something, which might make the parties concerned forget the matter completely. To achieve this end he ordered the people to move, although otherwise it was not the time of departure.

Orders for departure were given and the soldiers of Islam continued their march for more than twenty-four hours and did not halt except for prayers.[81]

Almighty Allah says with regard to this:

> *"They it is who say: Do not spend upon those who are with the Apostle of Allah until they break up. And Allah's are the treasures of the heavens and the earth, but the hypocrites do not understand. They say: If we return to Medina, the mighty will surely drive out the meaner therefrom; and to Allah belongs the might and to His Apostle and to the believers, but the hypocrites do not know." (63:7-8)*

Dishonesty and audacity of the hypocrites reached to such a level that they even hatched a plot to eliminate the Prophet of Islam (s). One of its examples occurred during return of the Prophet from the Battle of Tabuk, which was fortunately thwarted. After the conclusion of this battle, some leaders of hypocrites hatched a plot to assassinate the

---

[81] As-Seeratun Nabawiyya, Ibne Hisham, Vol. 3, Pg. 302; Majmaul Bayan, Vol. 10, Pg. 293

Holy Prophet (s) secretly. They planned to frighten his camel when he negotiated a perilous mountain cliff, so that it would rear up and stumble into the deep ravine.

The Holy Prophet (s) and his companions were on way to Medina. When they reached the top of the cliff, the conspirators decided to execute their nefarious plot. At this moment, Jibraeel came down and informed the Holy Prophet (s) about this conspiracy. The Messenger of Allah (s) ordered his soldiers: None of you must cross the cliff before me. Then he gave the rope of the camel to Ammar to lead the camel and also ordered Huzaifah to drive it from the rear and to control it properly. They set out after midnight till they reached the cliff. In a crucial passage, he saw a few riders who had concealed their faces and hid themselves in ambush. He said to Huzaifah: Hit the snouts of their mounts with your staff. Huzaifah attacked the enemies with his staff and dispersed their horses. Meanwhile, a hypocrite who was hiding on the mountain top threw a can filled with stones to startle the camel of the Prophet. But it missed the Prophet's beast and fell down the ravine. During these circumstances, Huzaifah and Ammar were controlling the camel of the Messenger of Allah (s) and they crossed the defile as soon as possible and were clear of danger. During these moments, the Prophet informed Huzaifah about the identities of the hypocrites.[82]

Even though hypocrites were considered Muslims, regretfully due to the effect of their internal disbelief they always had pacts of friendship and cooperation with disbelievers. In special gatherings, they supported the disbelievers and urged them to be firm in disbelief, to be determined in front of Muslims and to bear difficulties. They promised help and support to them, as the Holy Quran has said about the Jews of Bani Nuzayr:

---

[82] Biharul Anwar, Vol. 21, Pg. 196-231

"O you who believe! let not (one) people laugh at (another) people perchance they may be better than they, nor let women (laugh) at (other) women, perchance they may be better than they; and do not find fault with your own people nor call one another by nicknames; evil is a bad name after faith, and whoever does not turn, these it is that are the unjust. O you who believe! avoid most of suspicion, for surely suspicion in some cases is a sin, and do not spy nor let some of you backbite others. Does one of you like to eat the flesh of his dead brother? But you abhor it; and be careful of (your duty to) Allah, surely Allah is Oft-returning (to mercy), Merciful." (59:11-12)

Hypocrites were friendly to the Jews of Bani Nuzayr in a number of ways. They lent their support to them and urged them to remain determined against the Muslims and said: Be steadfast in your stance and do not fear the Muslims. We will support you and if they expel you from this area, we will also accompany you. And if they fight you, we would hasten for your help and assistance. But as the Holy Quran mentioned, the hypocrites did not fulfill their promise. When the Holy Prophet (s) signed a truce with Jews of Bani Nuzayr, under the terms of which, the Jews agreed to leave the Arabian Peninsula, the hypocrites did not keep their word and did not leave in their company.[83]

Hypocrites were dangerous persons as they created very serious difficulties and calamities for Islam. They exceeded the polytheists in their dishonesty and harms. That is why the Holy Quran paid special attention to expose their dishonesty. In many verses, Quran hints at their betrayals, falsehoods, mischiefs and conspiracies and warned the Muslims. Sometimes it has also threatened the hypocrites and said:

---

[83] Biharul Anwar, Vol. 20, Pg. 11-157; Majmaul Bayan, Vol. 9, Pg. 263

> *"If the hypocrites and those in whose hearts is a disease and the agitators in the city do not desist, We shall most certainly set you over them, then they shall not be your neighbors in it, but for a little while; cursed: wherever they are found they shall be seized and murdered, a (horrible) murdering." (33:60-61)*

It also says:

> *"..surely Allah will gather together the hypocrites and the unbelievers all in hell." (4:140)*

In the same way, it says:

> *"Surely the hypocrites are in the lowest stage of the fire and you shall not find a helper for them." (4:145)*

Again it says:

> *"O Prophet! Strive hard against the unbelievers and the hypocrites and be unyielding to them; and their abode is hell, and evil is the destination." (9:73)*

Presence of hypocrites and their deception was one of the difficulties of the Prophet of Islam (s) and the Muslims. Some of these same hypocrites were alive after the passing away of the Prophet and continued their betrayals and created a lot of difficulties in the spread of Islam. Even today they are involved in subversive activities against the spread and greatness of Islam and to destroy Islamic laws, rules of Quran and Islamic jurisprudence. Therefore, it is necessary on Muslims to recognize the hypocrites and to confront hypocrisy and hypocrites.

Unity of Islamic Ummah

Unity of Islamic Ummah

Almighty Allah considers all Muslims to be a single community and He says:

"Surely this Islam is your religion, one religion (only), and I am your Lord, therefore serve Me." (21:92)

The literary meaning of Ummah is a group of human beings who have a single aim in life and they cooperate with each other to reach their common aim.

Since Islam is concerned with reform and perfection of individuals, it is also attentive to society and its well being and success. The most important and necessary factor in formation of a permanent and strong society is unity in aim and cooperation in achieving it. If among the people of a society, unity and perfect cooperation is maintained, they can protect their social identity and independence and live in the world with confidence and self respect. But if they are disunited and dispersed, they would become humiliated, weak and wretched.

The Holy Prophet (s) said: A believer in relations to another believer is like a structure, whose different parts strengthen each other.[84]

Imam Ja'far Sadiq (a) said: By Allah, a believer is not a true believer, except that he is like the organ of the same body to another believer brother, in such a way that if one of the nerves is in pain all the other nerves also raise their cries.[85]

The Messenger of Allah (s) said: The example of believer in love and kindness with each other is like the example of a body; whenever one of its organs is in pain, all the other organs support it through sleeplessness and fever.[86]

The Messenger of Allah (s) was so concerned with the unity of Muslims that just after migration to Medina he established brotherhood between Muhajireen and Ansar and drew a memorandum of understanding beginning with the following:

In the name of Allah, the Beneficent, the Merciful. This is a memorandum of understanding from Muhammad (s) between the believers and Muslims of Quraish and Medina and those who may follow them and perform Jihad; all of them are one entity before other people.[87]

He did not rest content with this alliance and in order to strengthen unity between them he established brotherhood between every two persons. Ibne Hisham writes:

The Prophet of Islam (s) established brotherhood between the Muhajireen and Ansar. In this way, every two Muslims became brothers of each other. Then he held the hand of Ali (a) and said: Ali is my brother. In this manner, brotherhood was formed between all companions, which helped in the unity of Ummah. More importantly

---

[84] Sahih Muslim, Vol. 4, Pg. 1999

[85] Biharul Anwar, Vol. 74, Pg. 233

[86] Sahih Muslim, Vol. 4, Pg. 1999

[87] Seerah, Ibne Hisham, Vol. 2, Pg. 147; Al-Bidaya wan Nihaya, Vol. 3, Pg. 273

he declared that all Muslims, in every time and place are brothers.[88] The Holy Quran says:

> "The believers are but brethren, therefore make peace between your brethren and be careful of (your duty to) Allah that mercy may be had on you." (49:10)

Imam Ja'far Sadiq (a) said: A Muslim is brother of another Muslim. He is his guardian and guide. He is not dishonest with him and does not oppress him. He does not lie to him and does not backbite him.[89]

Commands and laws of Islam have been framed in such a way that they should assist and strengthen unity of the Ummah. For example, it emphasizes presence of Muslims in congregation prayer and Friday Prayer so that they may come together a number of times everyday and each of them becomes aware of the circumstances of others.

Imam Muhammad Baqir (a) said: One who leaves the congregation prayer without any legal excuse, in such a way that he has become aloof from congregation prayer and congregation of Muslims, his prayer will not be accepted.[90]

Imam Ja'far Sadiq (a) said: If one separates from the congregation of Muslims to the extent of even a span, he has forsaken the relationship of faith.[91]

Once in a year, Muslims of different Islamic countries of the world participate in the great and universal rituals of Hajj, so that they may become aware of the circumstances and conditions of the Islamic

---

[88] Seerah, Ibne Hisham, Vol. 2, Pg. 150
[89] Al-Kafi, Vol. 2, Pg. 16
[90] Wasailush Shia, Vol. 8, Pg. 292
[91] Wasailush Shia, Vol. 8, Pg. 294

countries and that they may find solution for their difficulties.

A great part of moral problems are arranged in a way that the spirit of cooperation and relationship between the Muslims is strengthened.

It is concluded from these lessons that Muslims are a single nation (Ummah) and individual Muslims are parts of that nation. Therefore, racial, lingual, communal, occupational, national and even religious differences are harmful to this unity.

That which makes the individual Muslims related to the great Islamic Ummah is follows: Faith in oneness of God, belief in resurrection and life after death, faith in the Prophet of Islam (s) and Quran. One who testifies to these points is a Muslim and is considered as a part of the great Ummah of Islam.

Muslims have same belief in many aspects of Islam. On the basis of this, if they have differences in some problems, it should not be a cause of discord and dissension between them.

The Quran says:

> *"And hold fast by the covenant of Allah all together and be not disunited, and remember the favor of Allah on you when you were enemies, then He united your hearts, so by His favor you became brethren; and you were on the brink of a pit of fire, then He saved you from it, thus does Allah make clear to you His communications that you may follow the right way." (3:103)*

All the power and glory that came into the fortune of Muslims in the early period of Islam was as a result of unity of word and single leadership.

Decadence and decline of Islamic Ummah started when they became disunited and got divided in different ways. Discord and opposition is one of the great calamities of nations. In form of a single nation, it can reach its possible perfection and achieve its aims as there is unity in it. On the contrary their power will be wasted and the community would not achieve its objectives.

The Holy Quran says:

"And obey Allah and His Apostle and do not quarrel for then you will be weak in hearts and your power will depart, and be patient; surely Allah is with the patient." (8:46)

The greatest problem and calamity, which still afflicts the great and powerful Ummah is discord and opposition. These difficulties have come into being due to the appearance of different Islamic schools of thought and sects. Self defeat and absence of independence of Islamic countries and domination of the enemies of Islam is only because of these differences. The great Muslim nation can escape these regretful circumstances only if it sidelines all differences and all Muslims unite into a single independent and powerful entity, which can solve its own political, economic, administrative and cultural problems.

Reformers and well wishers also should know that solving the general problems of the Muslim world is not possible, except through creating solidarity. Therefore, they must confront with factors of discord and should focus their views on one aim.

But unity of Ummah does not imply that followers of Islamic schools of thought and sects should give up their theological beliefs and jurisprudence and become followers of a single sect, because even though this is expected from them, it is not possible in the present circumstances, but its aim is that they should be true Muslims, observe common problems and overlook secondary differences. The following instances can be taken to be as common aims:

1. Promoting and propagating Islamic culture.
2. Propagating monotheism and confronting polytheism.
3. Defense of Islam, Quran and Islamic sanctities in front of the attack of international tyranny to weaken Islam.
4. Confronting the invasion of western culture, like the culture of materialism, sensuality and moral corruptions, absence of Hijab, unrestrained sexual freedom, profligacy and dishonesty.
5. Defending the usurped Islamic territories.
6. Confronting hegemony and domination of enemies of Islam in Islamic territories.
7. Defending the independence of Islamic countries.
8. Efforts to achieve economic, academic, technological, administrative, cultural and artistic self-reliance of the great Islamic Ummah.
9. Making effort to regain the greatness and power, which Muslim Ummah has lost.

The aim of the unity of Muslims and closeness between Islamic sects should create cooperation, concern for achieving common objectives and survival of the Islamic world. Muslim scholars are duty bound to guide the Muslims. It is through such unity that difficulties of the world of Islam would be solved and the greatness and independence of Islamic Ummah would be secured.

Mutual duties and rights of Muslims

Mutual duties and rights of Muslims

In view of Islam, all Muslims of the world form a single community, which should have its own heritage and distinctive quality. The great Islamic society is a single living human body. Although each organ and limb of man is having a particular responsibility, there also exists among them a kind of connection and cooperation in such a way that it bestows a special unity and is having its own special effects.

The great Islamic society is also one and Muslim individuals are in fact organs and limbs of this society. Every member of the Muslim community should assure that his well being and Islamic success is related to the well being and success of Muslim community. Therefore, independence and greatness of Islamic Ummah is not possible without support and fulfillment of mutual responsibilities of Muslim individuals.

That is why the holy law maker of Islam (Almighty God) framed mutual duties and rights for all Muslims, which are hinted in Quran and Islamic traditions. Below we present some examples from traditions:

1. Organizing the affairs of Muslims

Imam Ja'far Sadiq (a) has narrated from the Prophet of Islam (s): One who begins his day without having concern for the affairs of Muslims, is not a Muslim. And one who hears the plea of an individual, who says: O Muslims, and he does not harken to his call, is not a Muslim.[92]

2. Brotherhood

Imam Ja'far Sadiq (a) said: A Muslim is brother of another Muslim. He is his guardian and guide. He is not dishonest with him and does not oppress him. He does not lie to him and does not backbite him.[93]

3. Mutual rights of believers

Mualla bin Khunais says: I asked Imam Ja'far Sadiq (a): What right does a Muslim has on another?

He replied: Five rights are obligatory on him and if he omits some of them, he would go out of the pale of Wilayat and obedience of God

---

[92] Al-Kafi, Vol. 2, Pg. 164

[93] Al-Kafi, Vol. 2, Pg. 166

and God has no share in him.[94]

4. Love and Kindness

Imam Ja'far Sadiq (a) said: It is obligatory on Muslims to be cooperative, kind, supportive and affectionate among themselves. Since Allah has ordered it and said: They should be kind among themselves and aggrieved at the troubles of their brothers like the Helpers (Ansar) were during the time of the Messenger of Allah (s).[95]

5. Pleasing the believer

The Messenger of Allah (s) said: One, who makes a believer happy, has in fact pleased me and one who pleases me, has pleased Almighty Allah.[96]

6. Fulfilling the needs of believer

Imam Ja'far Sadiq (a) said: No one fulfills the needs of a Muslim, except that Almighty Allah tells him: Your reward is upon Me and in this regard, I am not content with anything less than Paradise for you.[97]

Imam Ja'far Sadiq (a) has narrated from Allah, the Mighty and Sublime that He said:

People are a family. The best of them is one who most kind to others and most concerned in solving their problems.[98]

7. Giving Advice

The Messenger of Allah (s) said: Muslims should advise their brothers like they are concerned for their own well being.[99]

In the same way, he said:

---

[94] Al-Kafi, Vol. 2, Pg. 169

[95] Al-Kafi, Vol. 2, Pg. 175

[96] Al-Kafi, Vol. 2, Pg. 188

[97] Al-Kafi, Vol. 2, Pg. 194

[98] Al-Kafi, Vol. 2, Pg. 199

[99] Al-Kafi, Vol. 2, Pg. 208

One who tries to fulfill a need of his Muslim brother, but he does not dispense good advice to him or is not concerned for his well being, has in fact betrayed the trust of Almighty Allah and His Messenger.[100] On the basis of this the lawmaker of the holy religion of Islam has paid special care for mutual relationships between Muslims and unity of the Islamic Ummah. He has advised those actions, which strengthen unity and has prohibited from factors which cause discord.

Some special qualities and responsibilities of The Ummah

Some special qualities and responsibilities of The Ummah
The Holy Quran considers Islamic community to be so important that Almighty Allah has chosen it and entrusted heavy responsibilities upon it. Although Prophet Ibrahim (a) requested Almighty Allah to create an Islamic Ummah from his progeny:

"Our Lord! and make us both submissive to Thee and (raise) from our offspring a nation submitting to Thee, and show us our ways of devotion and turn to us (mercifully), surely Thou art the Oft-returning (to mercy), the Merciful." (2:128)

He also says:

"And strive hard in (the way of) Allah, (such) a striving as is due to Him; He has chosen you and has not laid upon you

---
[100] Al-Kafi, Vol. 2, Pg. 362

> *any hardship in religion; the faith of your father Ibrahim; He named you Muslims before and in this, that the Apostle may be a bearer of witness to you, and you may be bearers of witness to the people; therefore keep up prayer and pay the poor-rate and hold fast by Allah; He is your Guardian; how excellent the Guardian and how excellent the Helper!" (22:78)*

Some important points are hinted at in these verses:

1. The coming into existence of the Islamic Ummah was due to the prayers of Prophet Ibrahim (a) and he named them as Muslims.
2. Islamic Ummah is the chosen one of Almighty Allah.
3. Islam is an easy religion and it has no hardship and difficulty.
4. Ummah of Islam would be the witness on the other communities, just as the Messenger of Allah (s) is the witness on Islamic Ummah.
5. Muslims are duty bound to perform Jihad to defend and propagate Islam.

The Holy Quran has mentioned some qualities for the Islamic Ummah and we hint at some of them as follows:

A – Almighty Allah has deemed the Islamic Ummah to be a medium nation, so that it be a witness on other people.

The Holy Quran says:

> *"And thus We have made you a medium (just) nation that you may be the bearers of witness to the people and (that) the Apostle may be a bearer of witness to you..." (2:143)*

Most commentators have interpreted 'wast' in the meaning of medium and moderate and said: Muslim Ummah is described as 'a medium nation' as it has legislated rules and regulations within limits of moderation and is away from excess and shortage. Islam neither calls man to extremism in materialism and sensuality, like apostates and materialists and nor does it calls to monasticism, asceticism, aloofness from worldly affairs and physical penance, as monks and ascetics in Christianity and Buddhism are. Islam has merged together world and hereafter, materialism and spirituality, spiritual and physical success and perfection and work and worship and has created a moderate limit.

There is no doubt that the existence of such a moderate Ummah is the best evidence of its capability with regard to social organization and assuring the success of the world and hereafter of man and it serves as an exemplar to all communities.

On the basis of this, the meaning of the verse becomes as follows: Almighty Allah has deemed you as a medium and moderate community, so that through the means of your moderate deeds you may lay an example of religious moderation in the view of the world and be a witness for others, just as the Messenger of Allah (s) is also a witness over you.

Therefore, Muslims should make efforts that by following the illuminated laws and commandments of Islam they become exemplars to others so that they may also be attracted to Islam.

B – Among other specialties of the Ummah of Islam is inviting others to righteousness, enjoining good and forbidding evil.

Almighty Allah says:

"And from among you there should be a party who invite to good and enjoin what is right and forbid the wrong, and these it is that shall be successful." (3:104)

He also says:

> *"You are the best of the nations raised up for (the benefit of) men; you enjoin what is right and forbid the wrong and believe in Allah..." (3:110)*

In the first verse, it is expected from Muslims that they should make themselves into a powerful nation and perform three important functions:
1. They should invite people to goodness.
2. They should enjoin good deeds.
3. They should forbid evil.

In the second verse also, three things are mentioned as the cause of this superiority:
1. Enjoining good,
2. Forbidding evil,
3. Faith in God.

On the basis of this, three great responsibilities are entrusted to the Islamic Ummah: Invite people to goodness, enjoin good and forbid evil extensively. That is why it is having precedence to all other communities.

Since the Islamic Ummah has accepted this important responsibility it should prepare itself for its fulfillment. It has the duty of calling people to goodness. It should be prepared to forbidding evil, extensively and in every situation. It should defend the rights of the deprived and poor, wherever they might be; it should confront the arrogant, oppressors and unjust. Although fulfillment of this extensive and important mission can be possible only in the instance that Islamic Ummah should be powerful and established in the fields of academics, economics, administration and technology.

C – Another distinctive quality of the Islamic Ummah is that it should be tough with the enemies and kind and flexible with Muslim.

The Holy Quran says:

> *"Muhammad is the Apostle of Allah, and those with him are firm of heart against the unbelievers, compassionate among themselves; you will see them bowing down, prostrating themselves, seeking grace from Allah and pleasure; their marks are in their faces because of the effect of prostration..."* (48:29)

In the above verse, two distinctive qualities of the Prophet and his companions are hinted at:

1. They do not accept flexibility and lenience before disbelievers and polytheists and in front of their hegemonies and trespassing. They are so equipped and powerful that they do not need conspiracies in order to get an upper hand.

2. However, they are affectionate among themselves. They consider all Muslims of the world to be the components of a single Islamic Ummah. They are happy with prosperity of their Muslim brothers and are aggrieved at their problems and difficulties. They make efforts for progress of Islamic Ummah and to solve social, political and economic problems of the Muslim public.

On the basis of this, Islamic territories should become determined against enemies of Islam and should not accept their force and domination. But there should be good and friendly relations between Muslim countries. They should defend the independence and territorial integrity of each other. They should cooperate with each other in all their occupations, they should avoid factors that create dissension and disunity and they should make the bonds of brotherhood and unity strong.

Part IV: Man in viewpoint of Islam

Man in viewpoint of Islam

Man in viewpoint of Islam

Man, in the view of Islam, is a multi-dimensional being. His creation began with a matter, which lacked perception and understanding and after traversing the stages of perfection, he developed into a being that is superior to matter.

The Holy Quran says with regard to the creation of man:

> *"And certainly We created man of an extract of clay. Then We made him a small seed in a firm resting-place. Then We made the seed a clot, then We made the clot a lump of flesh, then We made (in) the lump of flesh bones, then We clothed the bones with flesh, then We caused it to grow into another creation, so blessed be Allah, the best of the creators." (23:12-14)*

In the above verse, after explaining the stages of perfection of matter it is said: 'then We caused it to grow into another creation' In this stage, he has changed the words and instead of 'we created' the term of 'we originated' has been used. He has described this new creation in the words of 'another creation', that is the last stage of the creation of man is having absolute difference with the previous stages.

It is concluded from this verse that the last stage of the creation of man (form and soul) is superior to and more perfect than the previous stages.

In philosophy also, it is proved that the soul of man is an abstract being consisting of a matter, which is related to non-material effects. In the same way, it is proved that the material form, under the effect of the substantial motion (Harkat Jauhari), changes into a spiritual and non-material entity. Therefore, since this matter was extremely astonishing, Almighty Allah has praised this important matter in the Holy Quran and said:

"Blessed be Allah, the best of the creators." (23:14)

In another verse also, the story of the creation of man is narrated as follows:

"Who made good everything that He has created, and He began the creation of man from dust. Then He made his progeny of an extract of water held in light estimation. Then He made him complete and breathed into him of His spirit, and made for you the ears and the eyes and the hearts; little is it that you give thanks." (32:7-9)

In this verse, three important points are hinted at:

1. The soul is blown into the body of man when the body is perfected and becomes capable to accept it; which in Quran is described as 'made him complete'.

2. Allah, the Mighty and the High has related the soul of man to Himself and said: 'I blew My soul in it,' so that it may indicate the lofty status of man.

3. Man is introduced as a being that is in possession of ears, eyes, heart and soul. Since the tools of obtaining knowledge, that is ears, eyes and heart are placed in his being, he can obtain knowledge and gain precedence over the other creatures. This earthly and ethereal being, since he is having the above precedence, he became eligible to be the prayer direction of angels.

The Holy Quran also says:

> *"So when I have made him complete and breathed into him of My spirit, fall down making obeisance to him." (15:29)*

Man in Quran is described in two apparently contradictory ways: On one hand he is worthy of praise and laudation and is having superiority over all beings.

> *"And surely We have honored the children of Adam, and We carry them in the land and the sea, and We have given them of the good things, and We have made them to excel by an appropriate excellence over most of those whom We have created." (17:70)*

As a result of his special creation, man is capable of gaining knowledge, which cannot even be understood by angels.

The Holy Quran says in this regard:

> *"And He taught Adam all the names, then presented them to the angels; then He said: Tell me the names of those, if you are right. They said: Glory be to Thee! we have no knowledge, but that which Thou hast taught us; surely Thou art the Knowing, the Wise. He said: O Adam! inform them of their names. Then when he had informed them of their names, He said: Did I not say to you that I surely know what is secret in the heavens and the earth and (that) I know what you manifest and what you hide?" (2:31-33)*

On another occasion, He says:

> *"And when your Lord said to the angels, I am going to place in the earth a vicegerent, they said: What! wilt Thou place in it such as shall make mischief in it and shed blood, and we celebrate Thy praise and extol Thy holiness? He said: Surely I know what you do not know." (2:30)*

In these verses, man is introduced as a valuable being and the vicegerent of God on the earth and also a being that has such scientific capability that he is even superior to the proximate angels of God so much so that angels prostrated before his lofty station.

On the other hand, man is at the same time denounced in Quran and his evil aspects are also mentioned:

> "Surely man is created of a hasty temperament; being greatly grieved when evil afflicts him, and miserly when good befalls him." (70:19-21)

And He says:

> "..and man is created weak." (4:28)

And He says:

> "Nay! man is most surely inordinate. Because he sees himself free from want." (96:6-7)

> "And man prays for evil as he ought to pray for good, and man is ever hasty." (17:11)

> "...most surely man is very unjust, very ungrateful.' (14:34)

> "And if We make man taste mercy from Us, then take it off from him, most surely he is despairing, ungrateful. And if We make him taste a favor after distress has afflicted him, he will certainly say: The evils are gone away from me. Most surely he is exulting, boasting." (11:9-10)

> "Say: If you control the treasures of the mercy of my Lord, then you would withhold (them) from fear of spending, and man is miserly." (17:100)

Also, the two contradictory aspects of man are as follows: On one hand he is having an abstract ethereal soul, having the capability of obtaining knowledge, which is not possible from the angels. He is the vicegerent of God and angels have prostrated before him. Almighty Allah has praised him and made him superior over other beings. His nature is based on monotheism and it is aware of perfection. And on the other hand he is introduced as an oppressor, infidel, despairing, ignorant, riotous, anxious, obstructer, weak, hasty, gleeful, arrogant, niggardly and rebellious.

In traditions also, man is introduced in these same two ways. Now the question arises that what should be said in order to reconcile the two types of verses?

The reply is that man is a being with two kinds of natures, which is having two existences: half of his nature is from light and half from darkness. Although man is not more than one reality, he is having two dimensions: The aspect of bestiality and the aspect of humanity. On one hand, animal desires have been placed in his being and he is made the target of condemnation.

On the other hand, he is in possession of an abstract ethereal soul. His soul is a divine breath, which is compatible with and connected to the holy sphere and all the good deeds, merits, good manners and good qualities are all sourced from this; that is why he has been accorded nobility and became eligible that angels should prostrate before him. Man, as a result of this creation and specialties, can be attracted to animal desires and strengthen his bestial aspect as a result of which his human dimension would weaken. In the same way, he can focus his attention on human excellences and merits and to moderate and control the animal desires. It is at the discretion of man to choose any option he likes.

Man and Freedom of Choice

Man and Freedom of Choice

Man is a being, who is independent and has freedom of choice, because be performs his functions from the aspect of reason and intention. Man is not like a piece of stone, which is thrown up without any choice and which falls to the earth without an intention. It is also not like a tree, which absorbs nourishment from the earth without any intention, grows up and gives fruits. Man is also not a beast that acts due to instinct and has no self control over internal inclinations and selfish motives and that submits to inclination without thinking about the consequences.

On the contrary, the actions of man arise from knowledge and intention. He does what he intends to do. At the outset itself, he is aware of the advantages and disadvantages very well; then he decides whether to act or not; he chooses one option and fulfills it.

On the basis of this, man is a being that is independent and has freedom of selection. He always sees himself at the crossroads and considers himself to be free in choosing one option; that is why he contemplates on it.

One of the evidences of the freedom of choice of man is praise and condemnation of intellectuals. They consider some actions as good and praise the doer of those acts and they regard some acts as evil and condemn those who commit them. If man had not been free in his choice of his acts, positive and negative moral values would have been meaningless.

Islam also considers man to be independent and having freedom of choice. We have numerous verses and traditions with regard to this matter and we present some of them as follows:

The Holy Quran says:

"Surely We have created man from a small life-germ uniting (itself): We mean to try him, so We have made him hearing, seeing. Surely We have shown him the way: he may be thankful or unthankful." (76:2-3)

"...and whoever desires the reward of the hereafter I shall give him of it, and I will reward the grateful." (3:145)

"And say: The truth is from your Lord, so let him who please believe, and let him who please disbelieve..." (18:29)

"And whatever affliction befalls you, it is on account of what your hands have wrought, and (yet) He pardons most (of your faults)." (42:30)

"Corruption has appeared in the land and the sea on account of what the hands of men have wrought, that He may make them taste a part of that which they have done, so that they may return." (30:41)

"Allah does not impose upon any soul a duty but to the extent of its ability; for it is (the benefit of) what it has earned and upon it (the evil of) what it has wrought." (2:286)

"Surely they who deviate from the right way concerning Our communications are not hidden from Us. What! is he

> **then who is cast into the fire better, or he who comes safe on the day of resurrection? Do what you like; surely He sees what you do." (41:40)**

In these verses, the acts of man are related to his self and their consequences are also considered to be the results of his acts. On the basis of this, man in the view of Quran is a being that is free and having freedom of selection.

Traditions also clarify the independence and freedom of man.

Ibrahim says in a traditional report: I asked Imam Ali Reza (a): Does Almighty Allah compel His servants to commit sins? He replied: On the contrary, He has given them freedom of choice and respite, so that they might repent. I asked: Has Almighty Allah imposed on His servants duties that are beyond their capacity? He replied: How can He do this when He Himself says: "Allah is not unjust to the servants". Then Imam (a) said: My father, Musa Ibne Ja'far has narrated from his father, Ja'far bin Muhammad that he said: One who thinks that Allah compels men to commit sins, or that He makes them responsible to do that, which they are not capable of, do not eat the meat slaughtered by them, do not accept their testimony, do not pray behind them and don't give Zakat money to them.[101]

On the basis of this, according to the confirmed religious laws and testimony of intellectuals, supported by verses and traditions, man is having complete freedom in choosing his good or bad deeds.

At this juncture, it is necessary to hint at two important points:

First point: It was previously stated that freedom of choice is in the meaning that his actions are performed with sanction of reason and intention, but we should know that it does not necessary imply that acts and deeds of man are beyond the absolute and universal

---

[101] Biharul Anwar, Vol. 5, Pg. 11

laws of cause and effect and which are delegated by his own self. On the contrary, they also are having special causes that without their existence, actions and deeds of man cannot be performed. It is true that man is able to imagine the issue at the beginning itself, at that time he adopts it according to exigency, but the same attention and understanding of advantages and disadvantages and decision to do or not to do it, which are the prefaces of intention, will not be according to cause. On the contrary, perceptions, affections, internal inclinations, habits, views, family training, social circumstances and conditions and particular atmosphere of life and personality influence his style of thinking and selection. Each of them also in their own turn is the effect of its particular cause.

This chain of cause and effect also exists, so that divine will may continue in the same way; because the material world is created in this way and special laws have been made to control it. Allah desired that acts and deeds of man should be performed after contemplation and freedom of choice. On the basis of this, freedom of choice of man implies that his selection and intention is a part of the final cause of his action and the committing of act rests on him.

Second point: From that, which is mentioned, actions of man are connected to his own self and he has complete freedom in choosing them, it must not be concluded that actions are independently performed by man himself and that he is completely needless of God. On the contrary, since man is needful of the Glorified God in his existence and survival, in his acts and deeds also, he is needful of the favors of Almighty Allah. Thus if support of Allah is no more, there would be no actions or deeds as well.

That is why, in spite of the fact that actions of man are his own, sometimes they have also been related to God. The final activeness of God in this instance comes under the length of the activeness of man and not in its width.

Therefore, Almighty Allah says in the Holy Quran:

"And We did not send any apostle, but with the language of his people, so that he might explain to them clearly; then Allah makes whom He pleases err and He guides whom He pleases and He is the Mighty, the Wise." (14:4)

In the same way, He says:

"Say: O Allah, Master of the Kingdom! Thou givest the kingdom to whomsoever Thou pleasest and takest away the kingdom from whomsoever Thou pleasest, and Thou exaltest whom Thou pleasest and abasest whom Thou pleasest; in Thine hand is the good; surely, Thou hast power over all things." (3:26)

He also says:

"And if Allah pleases, He would certainly make you a single nation, but He causes to err whom He pleases and guides whom He pleases; and most certainly you will be questioned as to what you did." (16:93)

On the basis of this, misguidance and guidance, giving the kingdom and taking it away, giving honor and being degraded, all of this is attributed to Almighty Allah. Contrary to the previous verses, faith and disbelief, intention of reward of the world or rewards of the hereafter, performing good or bad acts, mischief in land or sea and the calamities that befall man, are attributed to man.

Although sometimes an act is attributed to God as well as to man, when He says:

> *"So you did not slay them, but it was Allah Who slew them, and you did not smite when you smote (the enemy), but it was Allah Who smote, and that He might confer upon the believers a good gift from Himself; surely Allah is Hearing, Knowing." (8:17)*

In the same way, He says:

> *"And you do not please except that Allah please, the Lord of the worlds." (81:29)*

Therefore act and will are also attributed to man as well as to God.

On the basis of this, there is no compulsion in action, as the acts are performed at the discretion and intention of man. Delegation is also not there, because the doer is not needless of the bestowals of God; on the contrary, it is a matter between the two, which in the terminology of Masoomeen (a) is introduced as 'Amrun baina amrain' (A matter between two matters).

When in the presence of Imam Ali Reza (a) conversation turned towards free will and destiny, he said: Shall I not mention to you a basic rule in this regard, so that you may never differ about it among yourselves and with which you may defeat your enemies? They said: Yes, please do. He said: Allah, the Mighty and Sublime is not obeyed through compulsion and is not disobeyed through force. He has not left His servants helpless in His kingdom. Allah is the owner of that, which He has given to the servants and He is powerful over that for which He has empowered the servants. If servants obey the command,

Allah does not obstruct them and if they want to commit sins and Allah wants to prevent it, He does so. And if He does not prevent and they commit the sin, Allah has not urged them to commit that sin.[102]

Muhammad bin Ijlan says: I asked Imam Ja'far Sadiq (a): Has Almighty Allah delegated actions to men? He replied: Almighty Allah is greater than that He should leave the actions of servants to Himself. I asked: Has he compelled people to their acts? He replied: Almighty Allah is more just than that He should compel His servants to commit an act and then punish them for it.[103]

Man and duty

Man and duty

Since non-living beings and vegetations are lacking perception and intention, they are not capable of bearing any kind of responsibilities. Animals are also not competent enough to bear duties and responsibilities, because they do not possess intellect, which may enable them to use contemplation and insight before their personal inclinations and to moderate and control their carnal desires.

Angels are also not needful of duties and legislation of commandments and laws, because their existence is superior to matter and materialism, they have no sensuality and anger that they should need to control them. Therefore, disobedience and sins can never be expected from them that they should be needful of commands and prohibitions.

---

[102] Biharul Anwar, Vol. 5, Pg. 16

[103] Biharul Anwar, Vol. 5, Pg. 51

Angels, with regard to duties, which are naturally imposed on them, are absolutely submissive to them and do not oppose them in any way.

The Holy Quran says, with regard to angels:

"...They do not disobey Allah in what He commands them, and do as they are commanded." (66:6)

It quotes the statement of angels that they say:

"And there is none of us but has an assigned place, and most surely we are they who draw themselves out in ranks, and we are most surely they who declare the glory (of Allah)." (37:164-166)

But man, as a result of his special creation, has accepted responsibilities and he can be entrusted with responsibilities, because firstly, he is not like the angels; on the contrary, his soul is related to the material body and through this it gains perfection and degradation; and obedience and disobedience can be expected from him.

Secondly: Man is a being that is created as intelligent and free and he is capable of reasoning and contemplation to discriminate what is good for him and what is against his interests. Man, as a result of these two special qualities, can be made duty bound and be subject to commands and prohibitions.

Abdullah bin Sinan says: I asked Imam Ja'far Sadiq (a): Who is superior, angels or human beings? He replied: Amirul Momineen Ali Ibne Abi Talib (a) said in this regard: Allah, the Mighty and Sublime gave intellect to angels without sensuality and gave the animals, sensuality without intellect; but He gave both to human beings. Thus, every person whose intellect dominates his sensuality, is better than angels and one, whose animal desires dominate his intellect, is inferior to the animals.[104]

The Holy Quran says:

> *"Surely We offered the trust to the heavens and the earth and the mountains, but they refused to be unfaithful to it and feared from it, and man has turned unfaithful to it; surely he is unjust, ignorant." (33:72)*

Some commentators have interpreted 'trust' to be the responsibility of bearing commands and prohibitions. In justification of this statement, it can be said: Allah, the Mighty and the High presented the duties to the earth and the heavens, but since they were not having the capability to bear them, they expressed helplessness in accepting those responsibilities. Angels of the heavens, also since they are not material and since they do not possess sensuality and anger, they were also not prepared to accept the duties. In between this, man alone was such that he had the capability of accepting the responsibility, since he is in possession of contemplation, discretion and intention, and is able to impose the limitations of divine laws on himself. Since man was unjust and ignorant that is he was prone to injustice and ignorance, he was able to accept the heavy trust of divine responsibilities. Becoming duty bound for man is a value, because as opposed to other created beings, for which the chosen path of perfection is closed, man was having this divine gift and the way of perfection has been prepared for him.

These duties are imposed by the creator of the universe, who due to His creation, is aware of the specialties of the body and soul of man and his well being and disadvantages of the world and the hereafter;

---

[104] Biharul Anwar, Vol. 5, Pg. 299

so He designed and framed these rules and sent them to human beings through infallible prophets. Since Almighty Allah was aware about factors of felicity and wickedness of man that is why He did not allow man to create this program for himself; He framed and designed the necessary laws and programs Himself and sent them to man through the prophets.

Although divine duties have to some extent, limited the absolute freedom of man, but this limitation is not against the interest of man. On the contrary, they are framed keeping his best interest in mind, because Almighty Allah can never do anything, which is harmful to His servants.

Basically, man cannot live in absolute freedom, since it is not in his real interests. Since man lives in a society and is in need of others, he has to accept social limitations as a result of which the limitations of religious laws also become applicable to him.

Quran says:

> *"(All) people are a single nation; so Allah raised prophets as bearers of good news and as warners, and He revealed with them the Book with truth, that it might judge between people in that in which they differed; and none but the very people who were given it differed about it after clear arguments had come to them, revolting among themselves; so Allah has guided by His will those who believe to the truth about which they differed and Allah guides whom He pleases to the right path." (2:213)*

Imam Ja'far Sadiq (a) was asked: Why has the Almighty Allah created man? He replied: Allah, the Mighty and the High, has not created man in vain and for no aim. He has not left them on their own wayward and without any control, on the contrary in order to show His power, He has created them in order to make them liable for duties, so that they may obtain His pleasure through obedience of divine commands. He has not created them to gain some advantage or to remove some harm from Himself, on the contrary, He created them in order to convey benefit to them and to make them inclined to the everlasting bounties of the hereafter.[105]

Duties of man

Duties of man

Duties, which are imposed on human beings, are wide ranging and are of different types, but the most important of them are the following three:

1. Duties of man to God and Prophet
2. Duties of man with regard to himself
3. Duties of man with regard to others.

Duties of man to God and Prophet

Man is logically and according to the law of religion duty-bound to recognize the creator of the universe and his giver of bounties. He thanks Him, worships Him and fulfills the duties He has imposed on him. He recognizes the true prophets, listens to the messages of God and gains through their guidance. Obedience of God and Prophet is in the interest of man only, because it secures for him the success of the world and the hereafter.

Quran says:

"O men! serve your Lord Who created you and those before

---

[105] Biharul Anwar, Vol. 5, Pg. 313

you so that you may guard (against evil)." (2:21)

"O you who believe! obey Allah and obey the Apostle, and do not make your deeds of no effect." (47:33)

"O you who believe! obey Allah and obey the Apostle and those in authority from among you; then if you quarrel about anything, refer it to Allah and the Apostle, if you believe in Allah and the last day; this is better and very good in the end." (4:59)

Duties of man with regard to himself

The dearest and the most valuable thing for man is his own self. It is necessary for man to before everything else, be concerned about his own self; that is: he should know what type of a being he is, from where has he come and where he is at present and what is his final destination? What are the causes of perfection and decadence?

Man should recognize his status in the world and be aware of his duties. It is necessary that he must think upon carefully where his real success and well being lies? What are the factors of his misfortune and failures? From where should he take the program of his life and how he should delineate his path?

If man thinks upon all this with full concentration and organizes the program of his life properly, he would make himself successful. If not, he has oppressed himself and cast his valuable self into destruction and what can be a greater loss than this?

The Holy Quran says:

"O you who believe! be careful of (your duty to) Allah, and let every soul consider what it has sent on for the morrow, and be careful of (your duty to) Allah; surely Allah is Aware of what you do." (59:18)

"Say: Allah (it is Whom) I serve, being sincere to Him in my obedience: Serve then what you like besides Him. Say: The losers surely are those who shall have lost themselves and their families on the day of resurrection; now surely that is the clear loss." (39:14-15)

"And guard yourselves against a day in which you shall be returned to Allah; then every soul shall be paid back in full what it has earned and they shall not be dealt with unjustly." (2:281)

"O you who believe! save yourselves and your families from a fire whose fuel is men and stones; over it are angels stern and strong, they do not disobey Allah in what He commands them, and do as they are commanded." (66:6)

Imam Sajjad (a) said: The right of your self against you is that you employ it in obeying God; then you deliver to your tongue its right, to your hearing its right, to your sight its right, to your hand its right, to your leg its right, to your stomach its right, to your private part its right, and you seek help from God in all that.[106]

---

[106] Tohafful Uqool, Pg. 262

Amirul Momineen (a) said: Self is a valuable gem, one who guards it, his rank is exalted and one who considers it unimportant, it takes him to baseness.[107]

He also said: One who has recognized his self; he does not drag it to baseness to the matters, which are destructive.[108]

Duties of man with regard to others

Man lives in society and is needful of the help and support of others. Human beings are compelled to live together and to cooperate with each other in social matters. Each of them has taken over social responsibilities. Human beings should observe the rules and regulations of the society, so that they may have a happy and comfortable life. Morals and social rights have also been framed and compiled in this regard.

Religion of Islam has paid full attention to social morals and has fixed upon each member of the society, mutual rights and advised and emphasized much on their observance.

Individual members of the society, who live in it, are having responsibilities; parents have responsibilities with regard to children and children have with regard to parents; husband and wife, brother and sister, neighbor with regard to his neighbor, teacher and student, scholar and ignorant, healthy and ill, ruler and subjects, officials and laymen, government officials and soldiers, old and young, Muslim youths to Muslims, Muslims with regard to People of the Book and disbelievers; all have mutual responsibilities.[109]

Although responsibilities of man are not fully clarified or limited as above; on the contrary, man is having responsibilities with regard

---

[107] Ghurarul Hikam, Pg. 227

[108] Ghurarul Hikam, Pg. 627

[109] Details of all the duties of man cannot be mentioned in this brief chapter; those who are interested may refer to the Holy Quran, books of commentary, traditions and ethics.

to animals, trees, rivers, atmosphere, environment, earth, mines and forests.

Part V: Duties, laws and their sources

Duties and laws of Islam

Duties and laws of Islam

Man requires a law in his social life, interactions and condition of relationships with others, occupation, professions and ownership, kinds of monetary transactions, marriage and family relations, securing social peace, rights of the individuals of the society, absence of injustice and oppression, prevention of tyranny and obstructions, punishing the criminals and opponents, guardianship and determination etc.

In the same way, in personal and inward life of man also, it is necessary that there should be a proper procedure of connection with the Lord of the universe, process of worship acts and rituals of servitude, recognition of the factors of success and misfortune, awareness of the good and bad morals and knowledge of method of development and perfection of the self is in dire need of the guidance of the Lord of the universe.

Since the creator of the universe was aware of the astonishing aspects and secrets of the body and soul of man and He knew about their different needs, he framed and designed the necessary laws and rules and sent them through the prophets. In the same way, he issued programs and necessary commandments to guarantee spiritual and ideal success, and sent them to human beings through the prophets. This collection has been entrusted to man in the form of a code of duties and explanation of responsibilities. That which has come to the people from God through the prophets is in form of rules and regulations or in the form of commands and prohibitions.

Laws and commandments of Islam, which are wide ranging and of different kinds are discussed and studied in books of traditions, jurisprudence, Quranic commentary and morals. Here, we would be content only to mention the classification of laws:

Laws of duty (Taklifi) and laws of situations (Waz'i)

Laws of Islam are divided into two groups: Laws of duty (Taklifi) and laws of situations (Waz'i).

Laws of duty (Ahkam Taklifi)

The laws of duty include those duties, which contain obligation, prohibition, desirability, undesirability and simple permissibility. Below, we explain each of them in brief:

Obligation (Wajib): A person, who is capable (Mukallaf) is duty bound to perform it and to omit it would make him a sinner and liable to punishment.

Prohibition (Haraam): A person, who is capable (Mukallaf) is duty bound to avoid it and to commit it would make him a sinner and liable to punishment.

Desirability (Mustahab): An act, performing which, is recommended and earns divine rewards, but omitting it does not make one punishable.

Undesirability (Makruh): An act, which in the view of Islam is detestable, but yet if someone commits it, he or she is not liable for any punishment.

Simple permissibility (Mubah): An act, doing and not doing which is same in the view of religion.

Laws of duty (Ahkam Taklifi) are called as such, because they impose duties on a person in the form of dos and don'ts.

Laws of situations (Ahkam Waz'i)

Laws like the law of marriage, property, ownership, freedom, slavery, guardianship, representation, conditionality, restraint, partiality, causality, evidentiality, validity, invalidity are called as 'Laws of situations'. These laws do not impose any duty or responsibility, on the contrary, they are issues, which Islam has framed and related various effects to them.

Laws of Servitude (Ahkam Ta'abbudi) and Laws of Mediation (Ahkam Tawassuli)

Laws of Servitude (Ahkam Ta'abbudi)

It means those things, the correct and valid performance of which depends upon the intention (niyyat) of proximity to God. That is, if the obligatory action is performed solely with the intention of approaching the Divine, without any worldly, material motive, it is correct and valid, and if not, it is not valid. Some servitude (Ta'abbudi) obligatory acts are: Obligatory Prayer, obligatory fasting, ritual bath after sex (Ghusl Janabat), ablution (Wudhu) dry ablution (Tayammum) for Obligatory Prayer, Obligatory circumambulation (Tawaaf), Obligatory Hajj, Zakat and Khums.

Recommended acts of servitude (Ta'abbudi) are: Recommended Prayer, recommended ritual bath (Ghusl) and ablution (Wudhu), recitation of Quran, supplication, devotions, recommended Hajj and Umrah, Ziyarat of the tombs of the Holy Prophet (s) and the Holy Imams (a) etc.

In all of the above, it is necessary that one should have sincerity of intention and his sole aim should be to gain proximity to Almighty Allah. If he or she performs any of these acts for show off, not only they be invalid, he or she is supposed to repeat them once more.

Laws of Mediation (Ahkam Tawassuli)

Any act, which is performed for another act and in which intention of gaining divine proximity is not required, is called as Act of mediation (Tawassuli). It is either obligatory or recommended.

Obligatory mediation (Wajib Tawassuli)

Like: Holy war (Jihad) in the way of God, defense of Islam and Islamic territories, defense of the oppressed, enjoining good, forbidding evil, fulfilling an oath, funeral rituals, repayment of debts, maintenance, reply to greeting (Salaam) and saving the life of a Muslim.

Such acts are obligatory mediation (Wajib Tawassuli); if they are performed with the intention of gaining divine proximity, they are rewardable and if they are not performed with this intention, they are not rewardable.

Recommended Mediation (Mustahab Tawassuli)

Such types of acts were themselves aimed at by the religious authority of Islam even if they are not performed with the intention of gaining divine proximity. So much so that if they are performed with the intention of gaining divine proximity, they carry rewards and if they are not performed with that intention, the actual aim is achieved although they would not earn any reward. Following are some examples of the same:

Cooperating in public welfare, doing a good turn to the parents, helping the weak, respect for the teacher, kindness to children, respect of elders, maintaining good relations with ones kindred, serving the public, solving the problems of people, fulfilling the needs of Muslims, entertaining guests, nice behavior with people, nice manners, pleasing the believers, visiting the sick, visiting Muslim brothers, teaching and training and propagating knowledge, taking care of the orphans, nice behavior with one family members, participating in Muslim funerals.

Universal and Sufficing obligations (Wajib 'Aini wa Kifai)

Another way in which the obligations are divided is into Universal and Sufficing obligations (Wajib 'Aini wa Kifai).

Universal obligations (Wajib 'Aini): Is that, which is obligatory on each and every individual, like prayer and fasting, Hajj, Zakat, Khums, etc. in such way that if one performs it, others will not be absolved.

Sufficing obligations (Wajib Kifai): Sufficing obligation is that, which is obligatory on some general Muslims, and which, when performed by one of them, is no longer obligatory on any of them. But if none of them perform it, all would be punishable; like in case of: funeral rituals, holy war, defense of Islam, enjoining good and forbidding evil, being involved in necessary occupations like: medicine, judiciary, agriculture, business etc.

On the basis of this, if one or some people cultivate these occupations according to the requirement, others are absolved from that responsibility. But if all omit it, or only if some cultivate it as are not sufficient, all of them would be culpable.

Specific and multiple choice obligation (Wajib T'ayuni wa Takhiyiri)

Obligations are divided into two groups in yet another way:

Specific obligation (Wajib T'ayuni): It is an obligation, which becomes obligatory to be performed specifically. Like: Prayer, fasting, Hajj, etc.

Multiple choice obligation (Wajib Takhiyiri): In this case, the duty bound person is given the choice to perform one of the two or more acts; like the penalty of not keeping a fast during the month of Ramadhan, which is either of the following three: To free a slave, to feed sixty poor people or to keep sixty fasts. The duty bound person can perform any of the three.

Prohibited acts in Islam, some acts are considered taboo and if one commits them he or she is promised divine chastisement. Like: To kill those whose murder is prohibited by Allah, adultery, homosexuality, oppression, usurping property of others, stealing, misappropriation, drinking wine, paying or accepting usury, eating unlawful animals, eating dead animals (animals not slaughtered in the Islamic way), looking at unrelated ladies, breaking oaths, making allegations, lying, backbiting, picking faults, paying and accepting bribes, consuming impure foods, fleeing from the battlefield (in Jihad), omitting obligatory duties and other numerous acts.

Such acts are introduced in Islam to be forbidden acts and Muslims are duty bound to avoid them.

Other laws

Laws of Islam are not fully explained in two groups: obligatory acts and forbidden acts; on the contrary they are extensive and they exist in every individual and social matter. We would only mention some general subjects as follows:

Impurities and Purifying agents

The following eleven things are essentially impure according to Islam and a Muslim is expected to keep himself pure from them; they are: urine, feces, unlawful meat animals, semen, dead body, blood, land dog and pig, alcoholic beverages, barley beer, infidel and sweat of an animal that persistently eats impurities.

Purifying agents: Purifying agents means those things which purify that which has become ritually impure. They are also eleven in number, the most important of them being water. It is not possible here to mention all the details, therefore those who are interested may refer to books of jurisprudence and code of Islamic laws.

Transactions

Laws of transactions are also extensive in Islam and we can only mention some of their general topics: Acquisitions, buying and selling, different types of charitable deeds, interest, right of mediation, rentals, contracts, gifts, endowments, proxies, foreign exchange, loans, partnerships, leases, payment of reward, lease land to a farmer, Musaqat,[110] agency, inheritance, bequests, mortgage, revival of wastelands, ownership, surety, bails, trusts, gleanings and usurpation etc.

Family Laws

Islam is also having detailed laws in the various sections of the family life of Muslims; and there are very specific and commands in some matters. We mention a few of them by way of example:

Marriage, dower, mutual rights of the spouses, nursing and laws related to children, maintenance, marital discord, divorce, waiting period after divorce, waiting period after the death of the spouse, etc.

Guardianship and rulership

Islam has also legislated detailed and extensive laws with regard to mastership and rulership; some of which are as follows:

Origin of Islamic guardianship and rulership; and the reasonings of its validity, description of Islamic rulership, requirements of the ruler, discretions of the ruler, duties of the ruler, process of selection of the guardian, duties of officials of the Islamic government, public property and government budget, taxes, Zakat, Khums, Jihad, judiciary, testimony, retaliation, penalties, blood monies, etc.

Laws related to foods and drinks

Laws like: Conditions of religiously lawful slaughter, the person who slaughters, conditions of hunting etc.

---

[110] Musaqat means that a person agrees with someone that for a specified time, the fruit-bearing trees owned by him, or those which are under his discretion, will be given to that person so that he cares, tends and waters them. In return, that person will have the right to take an agreed quantity of fruits. This transaction is called Musaqat.

Quran – fundamental source of Islamic laws

Quran – fundamental source of Islamic laws

Something from which laws and sciences of Islam are derived is known as the source and origin. These sources are four: Quran, Sunnah of the Prophet, traditions and life history of the Imams; and intellect.

The Holy Quran is the most important and reliable source of Islamic sciences and recognitions, because every Muslim has faith that this Quran was revealed from Almighty Allah upon the heart of the Prophet and no sort of distortion and changes have appeared in it. Therefore, such a distinction is not there for any heavenly scripture.

Distinction of words, meanings and connotations of Quran is also a clear matter. Even though the finality of evidence of the apparent form of Quran is subject to discussion, it does not need discussion and argument because:

Firstly: Quran is the program of life and a book of practical acts, which is revealed in a simple and eloquent language, which is understandable to ordinary human beings.

Secondly: Muslims of the early period of Islam, by hearing the verses, understood their duties and acted upon them and did not have any kind of doubt in it. The Holy Prophet (s) also, in his propagation, recited the Holy Quran to the people and reasoned through it.

Third: The Quran has also repeatedly urged people to contemplate and ponder on the verses and asked them to take benefit from them for their lives. In any other instance such contemplation would have been absurd.

On the basis of this, one should not doubt in the argumentation of the apparent aspect of Quran and relying on it and one should wait for confirmation of the proof. In order to prove it, some verses may also be resorted to:

Part V: Duties, laws and their sources

Almighty Allah says:

"*Surely this Quran guides to that which is most upright and gives good news to the believers who do good that they shall have a great reward.*" (17:9)

"*(It is) a Book of which the verses are made plain, an Arabic Quran for a people who know.*" (41:3)

"*O followers of the Book! indeed Our Apostle has come to you making clear to you much of what you concealed of the Book and passing over much; indeed, there has come to you light and a clear Book from Allah. With it Allah guides him who will follow His pleasure into the ways of safety and brings them out of utter darkness into light by His will and guides them to the right path.*" (5:15-16)

And He says:

"*These are the verses of the Book that makes (things) manifest.*" (12:1)

"*(It is) a Book We have revealed to you abounding in good that they may ponder over its verses, and that those endowed with understanding may be mindful.*" (38:29)

> "And this is a Book We have revealed, blessed; therefore follow it and guard (against evil) that mercy may be shown to you." (6:155)

> "Say: Allah is witness between you and me; and this Quran has been revealed to me that with it I may warn you and whomsoever it reaches." (6:19)

The Holy Quran has introduces itself with titles like: Light, Manifest Book, evidence, guide for the pious, guides to that which is most upright, gives good news to the believers, guides them to the right path, this Quran has been revealed to me that with it I may warn you and whomsoever it reaches, A Book of which the verses are made plain, an Arabic Quran, a Book We have revealed to you abounding in good that they may ponder over its verses, and that those endowed with understanding may be mindful. On the basis of this, it is not possible to have any doubt in argumentation through this book.

Some traditions also confirm the finality of proof of the apparent form of Quran:

Zaid bin Arqam said: "One day Allah's Messenger (s) stood up to deliver sermon at a watering place known as Khum situated between Mecca and Medina. He praised Allah, extolled Him and delivered the sermon and exhorted (us) and said: Now to our purpose. O people, I am a human being. I am about to receive a messenger (the angel of death) from my Lord and I, in response to Allah's call, (would bid good-bye to you), but I am leaving among you two weighty things: the one being the Book of Allah in which there is right guidance and light, so hold fast to the Book of Allah and adhere to it. He exhorted (us) (to hold fast) to the Book of Allah and then said: The second are the members of my household; I remind you (of your duties) to the members of my family, I remind you (of your duties) to the members of my family, I remind you (of your duties) to the members of my family."[111]

The Messenger of Allah (s) presented the Holy Quran as a reliable and permanent source of Islam, so that it would remain forever and will be useful for Muslims.

On the basis of this, Quran is the most important, most reliable, most trustworthy source of the sciences and laws of Islam and it can fulfill the cultural and religious needs of the community. Sciences and laws of Quran have originated from reality and have been compiled in accordance to nature, that is why they do not become outdated through the ages and as a result of progress of knowledge and human civilization, their value is not decreased. As much as the awareness of man increases and intellectuals ponder on this heavenly book, as much lofty meanings would they derive from it. We don't have any religious scripture, which has been so much studied as the Holy Quran and even then it remains worthy of further research and to derive more perfect matters and new meanings. A large number of books have been written regarding the interpretation and sciences of Quran, but there still exists scope for writing more detailed commentaries. Muslim jurisprudents have written detailed researches on the verses of legislation, but the door of jurisprudence and deriving solutions of problems is still open.

Since it is not possible to mention all those details here, we would mention only some of the topics of the Holy Quran and those interested in further details, may refer to books of Quranic commentaries.

The major subjects of the Holy Quran can be divided into a few groups:

1. Principles and fundamentals of belief, recognition of God,

---

[111] Sahih Muslim, Vol. 4, Tr. 1873

His names and His qualities, resurrection and life of the hereafter, purgatory and Judgment Day, scroll of deeds, accounting of deeds on Judgment Day, Paradise and its bounties, Hell and its chastisement, prophethood and need of sending the prophets, special qualities of the prophets, miracles of the prophets, conveyance of the message of God to people and the difficulties that they had to bear in this way, determination and initiative of the divine prophets in religious propagation, Imamate and guidance of Muslim community and qualifications of the Imam.

2. Stories, incidents and explanation of numerous efforts of the prophets in the path of religious propagation.

3. Encouraging people to adopt faith in God, resurrection and prophethood.

4. Glad tidings to believers and righteous persons of heavenly rewards and bounties of Paradise and warning the infidels and evil-doers of the chastisement of the hereafter.

5. Invitation to monotheism and confrontation with different kinds of polytheism.

6. Invitation to contemplation on the creation of the earth, heavens, stars, sun, seas, mountains, plants, trees, wind and rain, astonishing aspects of man and animals.

7. Reminding for the bounties of heavenly bounties and reminding how to recognize and how to value them.

8. Description of the believers and their good deeds, description of the disbelievers and hypocrites and their evil deeds.

9. Explanation of the circumstances of the past nations and their good or bad ends.

10. Discussions of the prophets with the people of their times within the subjects of monotheism, resurrection and prophethood.

11. Exposition of good morals and inviting people to them.

12. Mention of evil traits of character and need of avoiding them.

13. Miracles of the prophets.
14. Calling people to the worship of One God and urging them to perform the rituals of servitude like Prayers, fast, Hajj, Zakat and Khums.
15. Some political rules and regulations.
16. Some of the rules of business transactions.
17. Laws of inheritance and bequests.
18. Some laws of adjudication, witnessing, retaliation, penalties and blood monies.
19. Invitation to piety and discipline of the self.
20. Invitation to guarding of the self and controlling the selfish desires.
21. Explanation of some of the rules and problems of worship acts.
22. Condemnation of injustice and oppressors and mention of their terrible chastisement in the hereafter.
23. Paths of salvation of man and calling to it.
24. Factors of misfortune of man and warning about them.
25. Call to the unity of Ummah of Islam and prohibition of discord.

On the basis of this, the Holy Quran is the most independent and reliable sources of recognition of the laws of Islam, which can fulfill the different needs of people in Islamic societies throughout history. The Messenger of Allah (s) also left this valuable book as a gift among the Muslims and asked the Ummah to always remain attached to it and to take benefit of its commands and guidance.

Even though Quran is a book, which is very self sufficient, it does not make us needless of other sources of Islamic sciences like: Practice and life history of the Holy Prophet (s), traditions and biographies of the Holy Imams (a), because all subjects are not explained in Quran, rather only the general laws are mentioned and the explanation of their secondary matters have to be derived from Sunnah of the Prophet.

Two sources of the Sunnah

Two sources of the Sunnah

After the Holy Quran, the Sunnah of the Prophet is the most important source of Islamic sciences, erudition and laws. Sunnah has three implications: First: Statements of the Prophet with regard to religious matters and duties; Second: Action of the Prophet, which was performed in form of a religious act; Third: Silent approval or silence of the Prophet upon the action of one of his companions, which he performed as a religious act. In terminology, Sunnah also implies tradition and traditional report.

Traditions of the Holy Prophet (s) have played and till now play a very important role in explanation of erudition and laws of religion, because even though the Holy Quran is the most self-sufficient source of Islamic sciences, but in some instances it is needful of explanation and commentary, which are only fulfilled by the traditions of the Prophet and the Holy Imams (a). Some verses are general, absolute or abrogated whose specification, restriction or abrogation is not mentioned in Quran and traditions fulfill this need. It is an act of servitude, whose method of performance or parts and conditions or prefaces, secondary problems related to it are not mentioned in Quran and we are in need of traditions for their explanation.

Or, it is one of the comprehensive laws and whose exposition, interpretation and explanation of secondary matters are needful of traditions.

Basically, some subjects and laws have not come in Quran and have to be derived from the traditions.

The Messenger of Allah (s) has introduced the religion of Islam as a complete and comprehensive religion; which has concern for every dimension of the life of Muslims in the world as well as the hereafter and has framed laws for each and every matter; although from the verses, which have been revealed some fulfill this extensive need, but they were not sufficient. Therefore, the Holy Prophet (s) was appointed from Almighty Allah so that he may fulfill this need. In this regard, he also had the help of divine revelation. Muslims also became duty bound to obey the Messenger of Allah (s).

Quran says:

"O you who believe! obey Allah and obey the Apostle, and do not make your deeds void." (47:33)

It also says:

"Certainly you have in the Apostle of Allah an excellent exemplar for him who hopes in Allah and the latter day and remembers Allah much." (33:21)

On the basis of this, Muslims were duty bound to learn the beliefs and laws of religion through the Holy Prophet (s) and to obey his commandments and prohibitions. That is why Muslims paid attention to the statements and actions of the Prophet and what he said was accepted as a divine command. Method of performance of worship acts were learnt through his acts.

In this regard, some companions of the Prophet were more gifted in memorizing the laws and their rules. They got many opportunities to be present in the company of the Prophet and hear his statements; sometimes they also posed queries to him. When they were absent from there, upon their return they asked from their friends about the matters that were discussed in the meanwhile.

Muslims, who lived outside Medina, came to the city when they got opportunities and gained knowledge from the Prophet during some days. For example, Malik bin Huwairith narrates: I came to the Prophet with some men from my tribe and stayed with him for twenty nights. He was kind and merciful to us. When he realized our longing for our families, he said to us, "Go back and stay with your families and teach them the religion, and offer the prayer and one of you should pronounce the Adhan for the prayer when its time is due and the oldest one amongst you should lead the prayer."[112]

The Messenger of Allah (s) was always concerned about guidance of people and propagation of beliefs and laws of religion. He endeavored to propagate and disseminate religious teachings in Masjid, at home, in streets, bazaar and other places. In addition to the teachings of the verses of Quran, he also explained the matters to them. Sometimes, he taught them to others in order to perform religious rituals. If he noticed an improper act, he issued a reminder and explained its correct method. If they performed it in the right way, he praised them or maintained silence.

Jabir says: On the day of Eid of sacrifice I saw that the Holy Prophet (s) left his camel of conveyance and said: Learn the rituals of the Hajj from me, because it is possible that after this year, I may not get the honor of performing Hajj.[113]

In this way, the Messenger of Allah (s) endeavored to teach the beliefs and laws of religion and companions also paid attention to memorize and learn them. The Messenger of Allah (s) had two aims in this:

First: To make the companions aware of the beliefs and sciences of religion and to teach them the laws of duties of Islam.

Second: Recording and preservation of the laws of religion with aim

---

[112] Sahih Bukhari, Vol. 4, Pg. 52

[113] Sahih Muslim, Vol. 2, Pg. 943

to propagate them to the coming generations.

On the basis of this, beliefs of religion were recorded in form of traditions for Muslim and remained stored for them throughout the passage of centuries. Ali Ibne Abi Talib (a) was most active of all the companions in fulfillment of this great duty.

On this juncture, it is necessary to mention two points:

First reminder: Although, in sources of our reports there are many traditions, but it is not that every tradition should be reliable and worthy to be acted upon, because traditions are divided into two groups: Solitary reports and widely related reports.

Widely related reports: If a tradition is having a large number of narrators, in such a way that it is usually not possible that it could have been fabricated, such a tradition is called as 'a widely related report'. Widely related report (Mutawatir) is trustworthy and confirmed, because intellect and common parlance also act on this report.

Solitary report: It is a tradition, whose narrators do not reach to the level of 'widely related' (Tawatur): Solitary reports also are further divided into different kinds, like: Authentic, good, trustworthy, weak and chainless report.

Authentic report: It is a tradition, all of whose narrators are Twelver Shia and just.

Good report: It is a tradition, all of whose narrators are Imamites and trustworthy.

Trustworthy report: It is a tradition, all of whose narrators are non-Imamites and trustworthy.

Weak report: It is a tradition, some of whose narrators are weak and untrustworthy.

Fabricated tradition: It is a tradition, among whose narrators there reporters, who are fabricators of traditions.

Unknown tradition: It is a tradition, among whose narrators there are persons, whose life history is unknown.

Chainless tradition: It is a tradition, one of whose narrators has narrated it from someone directly, who was not his contemporary.

Authentic and good traditions are reliable in the view of scholars of jurisprudence and they act on them.

Trustworthy traditions are reliable, according to the view of the majority of the scholars.

But a weak tradition is unreliable, except that it should be accompanied with a context of authenticity or its weakness is compensated in a special manner.

Fabricated traditions are absolutely unreliable.

Second reminder: That, which is mentioned about the finality of the proof of solitary report, is related to traditions, which are narrated about religious duties and responsibilities, but traditions, which are related to fundamentals of belief, morals, natural science, history, matters of hygiene, special qualities of some plants, fruits, nourishments, drinks etc. are not evident legal proofs.

If solitary report is regarding matters, which require faith and certainty, like: Existence of God, monotheism, divine qualities, factuality of resurrection, originality of prophethood and need of sending of the prophets, it is not sufficient to be relied upon, on the contrary, one has to get faith and certainty through discussions and investigation.

Traditions of Ahle Bayt (a) – the third source

Traditions of Ahle Bayt (a) – the third source

The third source of the teachings and beliefs of Islam are the Sunnah and lifestyle of the Imams of Ahle Bayt (a). The Prophet of Islam (s) knew that after him, Muslims would be in need of a reliable and trustworthy point of reference in order to derive the laws of religion from it and that they might take refuge in it in solving their religious problems. With this aim he selected his Ahle Bayt (a) and introduced them to the Muslims, so that they may remain along with Quran and be the point of reference of religion. Time and again, he urged the people to refer to them, as mentioned in Shia and Sunni books of traditions.

One of the most important traditions is a tradition known as the Tradition of two-weighty things (Hadith Thaqlayn), which is narrated in different ways and in different versions; some of them are mentioned below:

Zaid bin Arqam says: When the Messenger of Allah (s) returned from the Farewell Hajj and reached Ghadeer Khum, he ordered that the ground under the trees be swept clean and then he said: As if I have been summoned by the Lord and very soon I would have to harken to the call. Indeed, I leave among you two things, one of them being greater than the other: Book of Allah and my progeny, my Ahle Bayt (a). Take care how you behave with them after me. The two of them will never separate, till they join me at the Pool of Kauthar. Then he said: Allah, the Mighty and Sublime is my master and I am the master of believers. Then he held the hand of Ali (a) and said: Of whomsoever I am the master, this Ali is also his master. O Allah, love those who love Ali and be inimical to those, who are inimical to Ali.[114]

In another place, he says as follows: I was present with the Messenger of Allah (s) in the Farewell Hajj. When we reached Ghadeer Khum, the Holy Prophet (s) ordered his men to clean the place under the date palms. After that he said: As if I have been summoned by the Lord and very soon I would have to harken to the call. Allah, the Mighty and Sublime is my master and I am the master of believers. Indeed, I leave among you two things, if you act on them, you would never go astray; Book of Allah and my progeny, my Ahle Bayt (a). The two of

---

[114] Mustadrak, Hakim, Vol. 3, Pg. 109

them will never separate till they join me at the Pool of Kauthar. Then he held the hand of Ali (a) and said: Of whomsoever I am the master and have right upon him, this Ali is also his master and is having more right upon him. O Allah, love those who love Ali and be inimical to those, who are inimical to Ali. Abu Tufayl says: I asked Zaid: Did you hear this directly from the Messenger of Allah (s)? He replied: Like all those who were present under the trees, I also witnessed that incident and heard the statements of the Prophet directly.[115]

Zaid bin Thabit says: The Messenger of Allah (s) said: I am leaving two successors among you: Book of Allah, which is a rope stretching between the earth and the heavens, and my Ahle Bayt (a); these two would not separate from each other till they meet me at the Pool of Kauthar.[116]

Huzaifah bin Usaid says: The Messenger of Allah (s) said: O people, I will depart before you and you would meet me at the Pool. When you meet me, I will most particularly interrogate you with regard to the two weighty things (Thaqlayn); so be careful how you deal with them after me. The greater of them is Quran, which on one side is in the hand of Allah and on the other side it is in your hands. Thus remain attached to them and do not go astray and do not make distortion in it.[117]

Abu Saeed says: The Messenger of Allah (s) said: I am leaving a thing among you and if you remain attached to it, you would never go astray and that is 'Thaqlayn'[118]. One of the two is greater than the other: Book of Allah, which is a rope from the heavens to the earth; and my Ahle Bayt (a). Know that the two would never separate till they meet

---

[115] Ansabul Ashraf, Vol. 2, Pg. 110

[116] Majmauz Zawaid, Vol. 9, Pg. 162

[117] Tarikh Baghdad, Vol. 8, Pg. 442

[118] Two 'heavy' things

me at the Pool.[119]

On the basis of this, the Tradition of Thaqlayn is a widely related (Mutawatir) tradition, which has been recorded in different versions through numerous chains through some personages of the senior companions of the Holy Prophet (s), like Zaid bin Arqam, Abu Zar Ghiffari, Abu Saeed Khudri, Ali Ibne Abi Talib (a), Zaid bin Thabit, Huzaifah bin Yaman, Ibne Abbas, Salman Farsi, Abu Huraira, Jabir bin Abdullah, Huzaifah bin Usaid Ghiffari, Jubair bin Motim, Hasan bin Ali, Fatima Zahra, Umme Hani binte Abu Talib, Umme Salma, Abu Rafe etc.

Imam Ali (a), during the period of his Caliphate one day recited a sermon among his companions and said: All of you who had been present in the event of Ghadeer Khum and heard the tradition of Thaqlayn from the Messenger of Allah (s), please arise and narrate what you heard. Seventy persons arose and said: We were present there and we heard the tradition from the Messenger of Allah (s). Some of those companions were as follows: Khuzaimah bin Thabit, Sahal bin Saad, Adi bin Hatim, Aqbah bin Aamir, Abu Ayyub Ansari, Abu Saeed Khudri, Abu Shuraih Khuzai, Abu Qudamah Ansari, Abu Yala Ansari, and Abu Haitham Taihan.[120]

Ahmad bin Hajar Haithami writes: The tradition of Thaqlayn is narrated through more than twenty persons from the companions of the Messenger of Allah (s).[121]

Three important points are derived from this valuable tradition:

1. The Prophet (s) has deemed Ahle Bayt (a) to be the equals of Quran and said: If you remain attached to them, you would never go astray. And I will ask you regarding this matter on Judgment Day. On the

---

[119] Musnad Ahmad bin Hanbal, Vol. 3, Pg. 59

[120] Yanabiul Mawaddah, Pg. 41

[121] Sawaiqul Mohriqa, Pg. 150

basis of this, as Quran is a reliable source of knowledge, Ahle Bayt of the Prophet are also points of reference and evident legal religious proofs and all Muslims are duty bound to refer to them in solving their problems that are related to religion.

2. As Quran remains as a reliable point of reference of knowledge among the people till Judgment Day, Ahle Bayt (a) also would also exist among the people till Judgment Day to serve as a point of reference.

3. Quran and Ahle Bayt (a) are two evident religious proofs, which would never separate from each other. On the basis of this, a Muslim cannot dispense with Ahle Bayt (a) and claim: The Book of Allah is sufficient for us, because no Muslim has right to dispense with Quran and only remain attached to Ahle Bayt (a).

Other traditions also are having the same meaning that following Ahle Bayt (a) is a cause of guidance and they consider aloofness from them as a factor for deviation. Like the tradition of the Ark.

Ibne Abbas has narrated from the Messenger of Allah (s) that he said: My Ahle Bayt (a) are like the Ark of Nuh (a). Whosoever boards it, gains salvation and one who does not board it, is drowned.[122]

Now, the question arises that who are Ahle Bayt (a)? Do they imply all the relatives of the Messenger of Allah (s)? Or it is those who lived in the house of the Prophet under his care; like his wives, consorts, children and servants?

It can be concluded from the text of the tradition that none of these possibilities is correct, because firstly the Holy Prophet (s) has deemed Ahle Bayt (a) to be equals to Quran and considered following them to be a cause of success and salvation and advised Muslims to obtain the laws of religion from them. Therefore, no one other than the infallibles (a) are learned in beliefs and laws of religion. Secondly: They should be absolutely free of sin and mistakes, so that following them leads to

---

[122] Majmauz Zawaid, Vol. 9, Pg. 168

perfect success and salvation. It is clear that all relatives of the Prophet were not thus.

On the basis of this, it is necessary that Ahle Bayt (a) are some particular personages. That is the same personalities, about whom the verse of purification is revealed:

"Allah only desires to keep away the uncleanness from you, O people of the House! and to purify you a (thorough) purifying." (33:33)

This verse informs us of the infallibility and purity of Ahle Bayt (a).

Regarding this, we have a number of traditions and some of them are as follows:

Umme Salma says: The verse: "Allah only desires to keep away the uncleanness from you, O people of the House" was revealed in my house. The Messenger of Allah (s) sent someone to summon Ali, Fatima, Hasan and Husain (a). When they arrived, he said: These are my Ahle Bayt (a).[123]

Umar bin Abi Salma, a ward of the Prophet, says: The verse: "Allah only desires to keep away the uncleanness from you, O people of the House! and to purify you a (thorough) purifying" was revealed in the house of Umme Salma. The Prophet called Fatima, Hasan and Husain (a), Ali was also with him; he threw his cloak over them and said: These are my Ahle Bayt (a) and Allah has removed all impurities (sins) from them. At that moment, Umme Salma asked: O Messenger of Allah (s), am I also not from them? He replied: Remain where you are; you are on good.[124]

---

[123] Mustadrak, Hakim, Vol. 3, Pg. 146

[124] Usdul Ghaba, Vol. 2, Pg. 12

Ayesha says: One morning, the Messenger of Allah (s) emerged from his chamber wearing a black woolen garment. Hasan arrived and went into the cloak; after that Husain followed and Fatima too; Ali also arrived and went below the cloak. Then the Holy Prophet (s) said: "Allah only desires to keep away the uncleanness from you, O people of the House! and to purify you a (thorough) purifying." (33:33)[125]

On the basis of this, the implication of Ahle Bayt (a) about whom the verse of purification is revealed, are the following: The Prophet, Ali, Fatima, Hasan and Husain (a).

But we have other traditions also that the Holy Prophet (s) has widened the scope of this term and introduced some other people also in Ahle Bayt.

Ibne Abbas says: I heard the Messenger of Allah (s) say: I, Ali, Hasan and Husain and nine persons from the progeny of Husain are free of sin and infallible.[126]

It can be concluded from such traditions that the implication of Ahle Bayt (a) in the tradition of two weighty things are Ali Ibne Abi Talib, Fatima, Hasan, Husain (a) and nine personages from the progeny of Imam Husain (a), who are introduced as Infallibles from Ahle Bayt (a) through the Prophet, Imam Ali, Imam Hasan and Imam Husain (a).[127]

On the basis of this, traditions of Ahle Bayt (a) and the Holy Imams (a) are the third source of knowledge and laws of Islam.

---

[125] Sahih Muslim, Vol. 4, Pg. 1883

[126] Faraidus Simtain, Vol. 2, Pg. 133

[127] The matter of infallibility and Imamate requires broader and detailed discussion, which at present is not possible; if in future opportunity is there, we will discuss in detail, Insha Allah.

Possessors of the prophetic sciences

Possessors of the prophetic sciences

The Messenger of Allah (s) was very much concerned for propagating the sciences and laws of Islam. Companions of the Prophet also made efforts to memorize the laws, but the Holy Prophet (s) did not consider this sufficient. He was well aware that the severe condition of the early period of Islam did not permit the Muslims to obtain the extensive Islamic sciences perfectly and to learn them by heart. He knew that companions were not immune from mistakes and doubts and there was possibility that by the passage of time, they would forget some of the laws or make them controversial.

It was therefore necessary that in order to protect the divine laws of Islam, they should be entrusted to a safe and reliable entity that is immune of mistake and doubts, so that Muslims may refer to them whenever they need. Hence, it was revealed from Almighty Allah to the Messenger of Allah (s) to choose Ali Ibne Abi Talib (a), since he was capable of bearing this important responsibility in every way.

With regard to this, Ali (a) says: The Messenger of Allah (s) told me: Allah ordered me to bring you close to me and commanded that you listen and remember. It is upon Allah that you listen and remember. Thus the following verse was revealed:

"..And that the retaining ear might retain it." (69:12)[128]

Ibne Abbas has narrated from the Messenger of Allah (s) that he said: When the following verse was revealed: "...and that the retaining ear might retain it," the Prophet said: I requested Almighty Allah to make

---
[128] Manaqib Khwarizmi, Pg. 199

them as the ears of Ali (a). Ali (a) says: I did not hear anything from the Messenger of Allah (s), but that I memorized it and never forgot it ever.[129]

In the same way, he says: When I came before Almighty Allah, He spoke to me confidentially; thus whatever I learnt, I taught it to Ali; thus Ali is the door of my knowledge.[130]

Amirul Momineen (a) says: Certainly, you know my position of close kinship and special relationship with the Prophet of Allah - peace and blessing of Allah be upon him and his descendants. When I was only a child, he took charge of me. He used to press me to his chest and lay me beside him in his bed, bring his body close to mine and make me smell his smell. He used to chew something and then feed me with it. He found no lie in my speaking, nor weakness in any act. From the time of his weaning, Allah had put a mighty angel with him to take him along the path of high character and good behavior through day and night, while I used to follow him like a young camel following in the footprints of its mother. Every day he would show me in the form of a banner some of his high traits and commanded me to follow it.

Every year he used to go in seclusion to the hill of Hira, where I saw him, but no one else saw him. In those days Islam did not exist in any house, except that of the Prophet of Allah - peace and blessing of Allah be upon him and his descendants - and Khadija, while I was the third after these two. I used to see and watch the effulgence of divine revelation and message, and breathed the scent of Prophethood. When the revelation descended on the Prophet of Allah - peace and blessing of Allah be upon him and his descendants - I heard the moan of Satan. I said, "O Prophet of Allah, what is this moan?" and he replied, "This is Satan, who has lost all hope of being worshipped. O Ali, you see all

---

[129] Manaqib Khwarizmi, Pg. 199

[130] Yanabiul Mawaddah, Pg. 79

that I see and you hear all that I hear, except that you are not a Prophet, but you are a vicegerent and you are surely on (the path of) virtue."[131]

Imam Ali (a) was asked: How is it that you have more traditions than other companions? He replied: When I asked the Prophet about something he replied to me; and when I was silent, he initiated the discussion.[132]

Amirul Momineen (a) said: "I would go in the presence of the holy Prophet once every day and once every night, when he would admit me and he would deal with me the way he wanted. The Sahabah, companions of the Prophet knew that the holy Prophet would not deal with others the way he dealt with me. Also the Prophet would come to my house most of the time, but when I would go to any one of his houses, he would admit me and would ask his wife to leave us alone and then we would have been the only ones therein. When he would come to my house, he would ask Fatima or any of my children to leave the house then whatever I would ask, he would answer me and when I would have exhausted all of my questions, he would begin from his side. Thus, nothing of the holy Quran has ever been revealed but that the holy prophet made me read it and dictated me and I wrote it down with my own hand writing. He taught me the interpretations of that verse and its explanations, its abrogating or that which was abrogated, the clear texts and the unclear statements, the ones of particular or general nature. He would pray to Allah to give me understanding and strong memory. I never forgot any of the verses of the book of Allah or any of the knowledge that he had dictated to me, which I wrote them down from the time he prayed to Allah for me. He did not leave anything of the lawful and unlawful, commands or prohibitions that were there or that would come into being in future or any book that

---

[131] Nahjul Balagha, Sermon 192

[132] Ansabul Ashraf, Vol. 2, Pg. 98

were revealed to anyone before him about the matters of obedience or disobedience that he had not completely taught me and I had not memorized them all. I have not forgotten of them even a single letter. The holy Prophet once placed his hand on my chest and prayed to Allah to fill my heart with knowledge, proper understanding, wisdom and light. I then said, "O messenger of Allah, may Allah take the soul of my mother and father in service for your cause, from the time you prayed for me, I have not forgotten a single matter or missed to write down anything. Do you fear that I might forget them in future?" "I do not fear for you any forgetfulness of ignorance." The Holy Prophet (s) replied.[133]

Ali (a) said: By Allah, no verse is revealed, but that I knew in what context, at what place and about what it was revealed. My Lord bestowed me with a perceptive heart and a speaking tongue.[134]

Some important points can be concluded from the above tradition:

1. Ali (a) remained with the Prophet since his childhood; so much so that he accompanied him even when he retired to the cave of Hira; and he emulated the Prophet in his manners and practice. The Messenger of Allah (s) was also most attentive to his training.

2. Ali (a) possessed considerable capabilities, he witnessed the effulgence of revelation, heard the voice of Jibraeel and the cry of Shaitan.

3. After proclamation of prophethood (Besat) also, the Holy Prophet (s) was commanded by Almighty Allah to bring Ali close to him.

4. The Prophet requested Almighty Allah to bestow to Ali (a) understanding, extraordinary perception and a hearing ear, in such a way that he must not forget anything at all. Almighty Allah also fulfilled

---

[133] Al-Kafi, Vol. 1, Pg. 64

[134] Tabaqat Ibne Saad, Vol. 2, Pg. 338

the request of the Holy Prophet (s) and He bestowed to Ali (a) powerful understanding and memory, in such a way that whatever he learnt by heart, he remembered it all his life.

5. Imam Ali (a), throughout the days and nights had confidential meetings with the Holy Prophet (s), in which no one other than him participated. That meeting took place at the residence of the Prophet or at the place of Imam Ali (a). The Prophet taught his knowledges to Ali (a) at the question of Imam Ali (a) or of his own accord.

6. In these meetings and in all instances when Ali (a) was in the company of the Prophet, he heard all the verses of Quran directly from His Eminence; wrote them down and also memorized them. He also learnt the sciences of interpretation and commentary of Quran etc. from the Holy Prophet (s).

On the basis of this, throughout his life, he learnt all points of religious cognition and laws of religion from the Messenger of Allah (s) and his blessed heart became a mine of knowledge and effulgence.

Ali (a) – a University

Imam Ali (a), as a result of his personal capacity and special supplication of the Prophet with regard to his training and education, throughout a period of twenty-three years of prophethood, obtained all the knowledge, cognition and laws of religion, all the verses of Quran and their interpretation from the Messenger of Allah (s) and became a treasure trove of religion cognition, as the Messenger of Allah (s) has clarified this time and again.

The Messenger of Allah (s) told Ali (a): O Ali, may you enjoy the taste of knowledge; you have crank knowledge like water.[135]

The Holy Prophet (s) said: I am the city of knowledge and Ali is its

---

[135] Usdul Ghaba, Vol. 4, Pg. 22

gate. One who desires knowledge should enter by the gate.[136]

The Messenger of Allah (s) said: O Ali, I am the city of knowledge and you are its gate; one who thinks that he can enter the city without going through the gate is a liar.[137]

Salman Farsi has narrated from the Holy Prophet (s) that he said: After me, Ali Ibne Abi Talib (a) is the scholar of the Ummah.[138]

Anas bin Malik has narrated that the Messenger of Allah (s) said to Ali (a): After me, you would explain the issues in which the Ummah differs.[139]

Abu Saeed Khudri also says: The Messenger of Allah (s) said: The best judge in my Ummah is Ali.[140]

On the basis of this academic comprehensiveness of Imam Ali (a) and his being the treasurer of knowledge of prophethood for the Ummah is supported by the Messenger of Allah (s).

The Holy Prophet (s) performed this important task with regard to Imam Ali (a), so that the knowledge of prophethood remained in a secure place and that after him it can benefit the Ummah.

Writing down of traditions

In spite of the fact that the Messenger of Allah (s) knew that Imam Ali (a) was immune to errors and forgetfulness in learning the laws of religion, he still ordered him to record in writing, all the knowledge and laws, so that it would remain available for future generations.

Ali (a) said: The Messenger of Allah (s) told me: O Ali, write down what I dictate to you. I asked: Do you fear that I will forget it? He replied: No, because I requested Almighty Allah to make you a

---

[136] Yanabiul Mawaddah, Pg. 82

[137] Yanabiul Mawaddah, Pg. 82

[138] Faraidus Simtain, Vol. 2, Pg. 97

[139] Mustadrak, Hakim, Vol. 3, Pg. 122

[140] Manaqib Khwarizmi, Pg. 39

memorizer (Hafiz); but you should write down for the Imams in your descendants.[141]

Imam Ali (a) obeyed the instructions of the Holy Prophet (s) and wrote down whatever he heard from the Prophet from the sciences and laws and also memorized them. Afterwards, the same books (writings) were transferred to other Imams as inheritance. One of the academic sources of the knowledge of Ahle Bayt (a) was that – as they stated on different occasions – it is written in the Book of Ali, or Sahifa or Jamia…

Bakr Ibne Karib Sairafi said: I heard Abu Abdillah (a) say: "In our possession is that, because of which we have no need of the people, but the people need us. And in our possession is a book, dictated by the Messenger of Allah (s) and inscribed in the handwriting of Ali (a) – it is a scroll in which is every permitted and forbidden thing is mentioned. When you bring a matter to us, we know if you will do it and we know if you will not do it."[142]

Abdullah bin Sinan says: I heard Imam Ja'far Sadiq (a) say: I have a skin (book) seventy yards long, which was dictated by the Holy Prophet (s) and is in the writing of Ali (a); everything that the people are in need of is present in it; so much so that it even mentions the penalty of a bruise.[143]

On the basis of this, one of the methods of preserving knowledge and laws of religion in the early period of Islam was by writing. That is why the responsibility of writing was entrusted to Ali Ibne Abi Talib (a).

After the sciences and laws of religion were transferred through the Holy Prophet (s) to the powerful memory of Imam Ali (a) and through

---

[141] Yanabiul Mawaddah, Pg. 22

[142] Al-Kafi, Vol. 1, Pg. 241

[143] Jame Ahadith Shia, Vol. 1, Pg. 10

His Eminence they were secured and preserved, the Messenger of Allah (s) introduced Ahle Bayt (a) as the point of reference of knowledge and called people to them.

After the passing away of the Holy Prophet (s), Ali (a) employed these two ways in the guidance and instruction of people. In addition to this, he also transferred his memorized and written sciences to his son, Imam Hasan (a). After the martyrdom of Imam Ali (a), Imam Hasan (a) in turn transferred the memorized knowledge and books to Imam Husain (a). In this manner, every Imam transferred the books to the Imam after him till they reached to the twelfth Imam – may Allah hasten his blessed reappearance, as the Imams have themselves explained, those books were one of the sources of their knowledge.

Jabir has narrated from Imam Muhammad Baqir (a) that he said: O Jabir, if we spoke to you from our personal opinion, we would have been from the destroyed ones. On the contrary, we only mention the sayings of the Messenger of Allah (s) that we have received.[144]

Some narrators of Imam Muhammad Baqir (a) heard him say: My tradition is the tradition of my father; and tradition of my father is tradition of my grandfather; and the tradition of my grandfather is the tradition of Imam Husain (a) and the tradition of Imam Husain (a) is the tradition of Imam Hasan (a) and the tradition of Imam Hasan (a) is the tradition of Amirul Momineen (a) and the tradition of Amirul Momineen (a) is the tradition of the Messenger of Allah (s) and the tradition of the Messenger of Allah (s) is the statement of Allah, the Mighty and Sublime.[145]

On the basis of this, the Messenger of Allah (s) chose his Ahle Bayt (a), who are immune from mistake and forgetfulness, for the purpose of preserving the sciences and laws of religion. Therefore he entrusted

---

[144] Jame Ahadith Shia, Vol. 1, Pg. 13

[145] Al-Kafi, Vol. 1, Pg. 53

the sciences of prophethood to them in two ways: through verbal instruction and memorization and through writing and reliable books. The Holy Imams (a) and Ahle Bayt (a) of the Prophet also transferred this in two ways: One, through quoting them from their forefathers and another by quoting from the books they had inherited from the Messenger of Allah (s). In any case, it was considered to be the most reliable way of narrating traditions.

Thus, according to the tradition of two weighty things and similar traditions, it is obligatory on Muslims to refer to them in obtaining the knowledge of religion.[146]

Reason is the fourth source

Reason is the fourth source

Reason can be considered to be the fourth source of sciences and laws of religion. The most important distinction of man over animals is intellect or reason. Civilization and progress in natural sciences, technology, humanities, philosophy, Gnosticism, ethics, arts etc. are all contributions of the intellect of man. If reason and intellectual sources are taken away from man, he would lose all these perfections. Basically, the daily life of man is based on these same intellectual sources.

In Islamic culture also, intellect is introduced as a prominent and valuable entity, which can lead man in exposing realities. Islam is a religion of contemplation, rationalization and reason.

---

[146] It is said that the sciences of the Infallible Imams (a) are not restricted to these two ways, on the contrary, they have other ways as well, whose mention is not presently possible.

The Holy Quran in numerous verses has invited people to contemplation, pondering and reasoning and has condemned its absence:

"Most surely in the creation of the heavens and the earth and the alternation of the night and the day, and the ships that run in the sea with that which profits men, and the water that Allah sends down from the cloud, then gives life with it to the earth after its death and spreads in it all (kinds of) animals, and the changing of the winds and the clouds made subservient between the heaven and the earth, there are signs for a people who understand." (2:164)

He also says:

"And He it is, Who made for you the ears and the eyes and the hearts; little is it that you give thanks. And He it is, Who multiplied you in the earth, and to Him you shall be gathered. And He it is, Who gives life and causes death, and (in) His (control) is the alternation of the night and the day; do you not then understand?" (23:78-80)

Numerous traditions have been recorded about the importance of intellect, reason and contemplation. The first topic of Al-Kafi is 'The Book of Reason and Ignorance'. It is mentioned in it:

Abdullah bin Sinan has narrated from Imam Ja'far Sadiq (a) that he said: The Prophet is the proof of Allah on the people and reason is the proof between Allah and the people.[147]

In the same way, he said: Reason is the guide of believers.[148]

The Holy Quran, in addition to inviting the people to contemplation and pondering, has itself resorted to logical reasonings in many instances. The Prophet of Islam (s) and the Holy Imams (a) invited people to contemplate and proved their points through logical reasoning.

On the basis of this, the method of using reason and logical argumentation became acceptable in Islam and it urged people to follow this method. Therefore, reason became a reliable religious proof and a source of sciences and laws. It is possible to reach to the realities through intellect and logical reasoning. If intellectual sources are according to the criteria, they expose the reality and produce certainty. Although it is also not in the meaning that intellect in its own understanding, is basically free of error and its perceptions are always according to the situation, because existence of instances of mistake cannot be denied, but existence of limited instances of errors do not harm the root of the intellectual laws and do not dismiss intellect from the position of the finality of evidence. On the contrary, the cause of occurrence of these errors should be searched for in incorrect method of contemplation and reasoning. It is due to this that the science of logic has been developed

Use of intellect

It is correct that intellect is a trustworthy and honest guide and it can be used to expose the realities, but it is not correct that we should wait for logical reasoning in proving every matter; on the contrary there are laws and judgments in special cases, which are briefly as follows:

Logical reasoning in fundamentals of belief

---

[147] Al-Kafi, Vol. 1, Pg. 25

[148] Al-Kafi, Vol. 1, Pg. 25

Religious beliefs can be divided into two groups: Fundamentals of beliefs (Roots of religion) and secondary beliefs (Branches of religion).

In Fundamentals of beliefs (Roots of religion), it is allowed to make use of logical reasoning; like in case of proving the existence of God; monotheism, positive and negative divine attributes, proving resurrection, necessity of sending of the prophets, proving the infallibility and knowledge of prophets, proving the origin of Imamate and necessity of appointment of the Imams and proving the knowledge and infallibility of the Imam.

In all the absolute fundamentals of belief, it is possible to make use of logical reasoning; that is why it is necessary to believe in those points of belief only after proper reasoning and contemplation. Islam in no way compels people to accept the fundamentals of belief without logical reasoning; on the contrary, it has urged them to ponder and comptemplate.

But in secondary beliefs, mostly there is no scope for logical reasoning, like the existence of purgatory, interrogation of the grave, process of establishment of Judgment Day, proving of deeds, accounting of deeds, balance of deeds, Sirat Bridge, true description of bounties of Paradise and chastisement of Hell etc. On the basis of this, it is not possible to understand these realities through intellect and logical reasoning alone; on the contrary, in these matters, it is necessary to rely on reliable religious texts. Same is the case with regard to the intercession of prophets, Imams and holy saints, existence of angels, existence of Shaitan and how he dominates human beings; the process of divine revelation; all these cannot be understood through logical reasoning alone, on the contrary, it is necessary to refer to religious traditional reports.

Logical reasoning in practical laws

It is also possible to use logical reasoning in deriving some practical obligatory laws. For example in the following instances:

First: Deriving the religious command in a subject from criterion and definite philosophy of a law in another subject; for example, there is an issue in scholastic theology believed in by most Muslims, especially Shia Imamiyah; and it is that laws of Shariah are framed keeping the real merits and demerits of a thing. That is if something is obligatory or prohibited in religious law, it is so because it is in fact necessary or harmful. In the same way, if something is recommended or detestable, it is because it is having an inherent merit or a demerit.

On the basis of this, if the legislator has framed law on a subject along with a cause, and intellect also creates the same cause in another topic, it necessitates that the second topic is also having the first command, even though it might not have reached us.

For example, the law maker says: Do not take wine, since it intoxicates. Now if intellect comes to know about the intoxicating qualities of other drinks, like Nabidh[149] etc. it can declare that Nabidh is also prohibited. That is according to intellectual requirement, it says: 'All that is ordered by intellect is also commanded by Shariah'. Therefore, it prohibits Nabidh also even though this command might not have reached us.

In the same way, if intellect finds a defect in an action, it orders against it. In that instance, according to requirement of intellect, it would be said that the legislator has also in this instance issued prohibition about it, because the legislator with regard to His servants, does not revoke any exigency. For example, if reason perceives that use of narcotics, like heroin is having individual and social ills, it orders against this act. In that instance, according to the rule of requirement of intellect, it would be said that addiction and use of heroin is also unlawful according the law of religion.

---

[149] Date wine

On the basis of this, in such instances, it is possible to conclude a religious command from logic; hence logic is a method of deriving a religious command.

Although the rule of requirement of intellect will be applicable in the instance and in the process of deriving the law of religion, it is determined that criterion and actual cause of the law, by the reliable legal reasoning should have been proved, or the existence of exigency or evil should have been proved from the definite law of intellect, but it is not possible to derive the law of Shariah through logical analogy and lenient interpretation.

Anyway, such derivation cannot be made by anyone except by a jurist, who is aware of the time, place and contemporary conditions.

Second: Conflict of two obligatory duties: For example, on one side the time of prayer is tight and only enough time is left to perform the obligatory part; on the other hand, a believer is drowning; in such a case, two obligatory duties have come upon one person: Both, performance of prayer and saving the life of a believer are obligatory; but he cannot fulfill both, and he is compelled to choose one. On this juncture, reason commands that saving the life of a believer is more important than prayer; thus he must give priority to it even if his prayer may lapse.

Third: Obligation of performing the prefaces of obligatory acts; that is if the act becomes obligatory, reason commands: It is obligatory for the obliged person to prepare the prefaces of that act, so that he may be able to perform the obligatory duty. For example, if Hajj is obligatory on a person, reason orders him to prepare the preliminaries of the journey and to travel to Mecca, so that he may wear the pilgrim garb at Miqaat[150] and perform the obligatory rituals of Hajj. Completing the formalities is obligatory according to reason even if the Law Maker may not have specified it.

---

[150] Starting point of Hajj

On the basis of this, reason is also a source of sciences and laws of Islam; with regard to fundamentals of belief, reason is having a decisive say and in deriving the laws also in its special instances, it becomes useful to the jurisprudents.

Ijtihad and Taqlid

Ijtihad and Taqlid

Ijtihad literary means effort and its terminological meaning is: Making effort in deriving the laws of Shariah from the authorized reliable sources like Quran, traditions of the Prophet, traditions of the Holy Imams (a), reason, principles of practice and fundamental laws, whose finality of proof has been proved through legal reasoning.

On the basis of this, Ijtihad is not a part of sources of Shariah; on the contrary it is a means of deriving the laws from religious sources.

During the lifetime of the Messenger of Allah (s), Ijtihad did not exist in the present form and there was no need of it, because Muslims had direct access to the Prophet and through direct or indirect contact got the solutions of their problems. This period is known as the period of legislation.

From the tenure of Imamate of Imam Ali (a) till the time of the martyrdom of Imam Hasan Askari (a) also, there was not at all any need of Ijtihad, because people were having access to the Holy Imams (a) and the bearers of prophetic sciences. Followers of Ahle Bayt (a) directly or indirectly established contact with the Holy Imams (a) and inquired about the solutions of their problems. During this period, the Holy Imams (a) put in most efforts to propagate the fundamentals of belief and laws of religion. Their companions also tried their best to preserve and propagate the traditions. By the blessings of efforts of the Holy Imams (a) and through the endeavor of companions, Shia culture became popular and Shia became very self-sufficient from the aspect of beliefs and laws of religion. Hundreds of books were compiled on different subjects. In the period of Imam Muhammad Baqir and Imam Ja'far Sadiq (a), the holy city of Medina became a university of Islamic knowledge, where different kinds of religious sciences were taught and from there they were issued to the other centers of Shiaism. During this bountiful period, thousands of intellectuals were trained who made efforts in propagating the sciences of Ahle Bayt (a).

In the presence of these possibilities Shia did not have any need of Ijtihad at all, but at the same time there existed among the narrators of traditions, jurisprudents whom others referred to in secondary legal matters. These persons were owners of opinion and verdict and their views became known among the companions and writers; like Yunus bin Abdur Rahman and Zurarah etc.[151]

The Holy Imams (a) also encouraged and supported them in various ways. When a man from Syria said to Imam Ja'far Sadiq (a): I have come to debate with you about jurisprudence. Imam (a) said to Zurarah: Have a debate with this man about jurisprudence.[152] Imam Muhammad Baqir (a) said to Aban Taghlib: Sit in the Masjid of Medina and issue verdicts to public, because I like to see persons like you among Shia.[153]

Imam Ja'far Sadiq (a) says: It is our duty to explain the fundamentals to you and it is your duty to derive the secondary laws from them.[154] It is known that the Holy Imams (a) paid special attention to necessary

---

[151] Al-Kafi, Vol. 7, Pg. 83

[152] Qamusar Rijal, Vol. 4, Pg. 156

[153] Qamusar Rijal, Vol. 4, Pg. 73

[154] Wasailush Shia, Vol. 27, Pg. 61

requirements of jurisprudence. As a result of their concern and efforts of companions, a number of Islamic jurisprudents (Mujtahids) came into being, who wrote books on jurisprudence and answered queries of people. Some of their names and the books they have authored are mentioned in Fehrist Ibne Nadeem.[155]

Even though during the period of Imamate, among the companions of the Holy Imams (a), there existed jurisprudents who had reached to the level of Ijtihad, however referring to the Imams and directly referring to them had priority.

But in the period of the minor occultation, the circumstances of Shia Imamiyah changed, because on one hand the number of Shia had increased in cities and towns of the country, on the other hand the general circumstances of people had undergone a change and new religious problems had appeared which needed solutions. But regrettably, the Twelfth Imam had disappeared and there was no possibility for Shia to contact him directly, except through the four deputies of the Imam, who were appointed to this post one after another throughout this period of Imamate. These contacts also didn't reach to such a level that they should be sufficient to fulfill the extensive and different needs of Shia.

In this period, there was need of scholars and great jurisprudents who through their knowledge and Ijtihad may fill the void during the occultation of the Imam and derive and convey to them the needed solutions of widespread problems from the sources of jurisprudence through the process of Ijtihad, and that they serve as points of reference and defend the existence of Shiaism. Existence of such intellectuals for the sake of providing a point of reference in the matter of faith for the Shia youth was very much needed and which gradually developed by the grace of God.

---

[155] Fehrist Ibne Nadeem, Pg 317-328

A great scholar of that period was Ali bin Husain bin Musa bin Babawayh Qummi. This great jurisprudent was born in the beginning period of the Minor Occultation. He lived during the tenure of three special deputies of the Imam Zamana (a). He met Husain bin Ruh, the third deputy of Imam Zamana (a) in 328 A.H. and passed away in 329 A.H. in Qom, and his grave is situated at the same place. At that time, he was the point of reference and a prominent face of Shiaism. He wrote numerous books on different sciences; like for example: Sharai, a book on jurisprudence. This scholar rendered valuable services to the Shia.[156]

After him, his son, Muhammad bin Ali bin Husain bin Babawayh, alias Saduq was a jurisprudent and authoritative Shia scholar. He also wrote books on various subjects, including jurisprudence; like for example: Muqna, Man Laa Yahzaharul Faqih etc. This great jurisprudent also lived in Qom. He spent a period in Baghdad as well, in pursuit of knowledge. In his final years, he resided in the city of Rayy and passed away in the year 381 A.H. and his grave is situated there.[157]

These two important jurisprudents mostly based their legal judgments on traditions.

Another jurisprudent, who lived at the end of the period of the Minor Occultation and the beginning period of the Major Occultation was Hasan bin Ali bin Abi Aqeel Omani. He was a great jurisprudential scholar, who was a Shia point of reference during his lifetime and he disseminated the sciences of Ahle Bayt (a) through his speeches and writings. This great and important scholar wrote a large number of books on different sciences, like jurisprudence; the most important of

---

[156] Bahjatul Amaal, Vol. 5, Pg. 416

[157] Bahjatul Amaal, Vol. 6, Pg. 495

them being: Al Mustamsik bi Habli Aali Rasool.[158]

Muhammad bin Ahmad bin Junaid Iskafi also lived during the early period of the Major Occultation. It seems that this great jurist also lived for sometime during the period of the Minor Occultation. He is a scholar and jurisprudent of the fourth century. He has written numerous books on different subjects and one of his works on jurisprudence is: Tahdhibu Shia Li Ahkamul Shariah.[159]

Ibne Junaid followed the style of Omani in deriving the laws of Shariah. These two great jurisprudents were the true founders of Ijtihad. They also employed reason in deriving the laws of Shariah; and they have contributed to all the sources and dimensions of subjects and problems.[160]

It was this style of Ijtihad, which was followed and perfected by Shaykh Mufeed (336-381 A.H.) one of the prominent disciples of Ibne Junaid. One of the jurisprudential writings of Shaykh Mufeed is Kitab Muqna, which has fortunately survived the upheavals of time and which is useful for those who are interested.

After Mufeed, Sayyid Murtaza (died 436 A.H.) wrote Intisar and Nasiryaat and Salar bin Abdul Aziz (died 463 A.H.) wrote Kitab Marasim on the method of Ijtihad.

Most important of all, Shaykhut Taifah, Muhammad bin Hasan Tusi (385-460 A.H.) made efforts and displayed initiative in the reformation and perfection of the method of Ijtihad. He studied under Shaykh Mufeed and Sayyid Murtaza for 23 years in Baghdad and after them succeeded to the post of final point of reference (Maraja) and leadership of Shia. After the tragical events of Baghdad, he moved to Najaf and laid the foundation of the religious university of Najaf. He is the author of

---

[158] Bahjatul Amaal, Vol. 3, Pg. 150-154
[159] Bahjatul Amaal, Vol. 6, Pg. 241-250
[160] Bahjatul Amaal, Vol. 3, Pg. 150-154

books like, Khilaf, Tadkira and Mabsut on the subject of jurisprudence. Shaykh Tusi was the first of those who designed the Shia reasoning of jurisprudence in an extensive form and derived laws from fundamental principles.

Jurists after the Shaykh also in improving and compiling of jurisprudence and science of principles, which are the sources of deriving the laws of Shariah, made efforts for years so that Ijtihad may take an extensive and detailed form.

Requirements of Ijtihad

Science of jurisprudence and its principles developed gradually till it assumed the present shape. Therefore, Ijtihad and deriving the laws is a cumbersome job having great responsibilities, which requires much preparation and specialization. Following are the necessary requirements for being an Islamic jurist (Mujtahid):

1. Specialization in sciences related to the deriving of the laws; like Arabic language and grammar, knowledge of traditions, identification of narrators of traditions, science of Quranic commentary, complete and perfect command on traditions of the Prophet and the Holy Imams (a); specialization in science of the principles of jurisprudence and having clear sources of principles.

2. Intelligence, liberal mindedness and valor in expression of truth.

3. Awareness of progress of sciences and technology and their effect on circumstances and on individual and social, political and economic conditions of the Muslim Ummah.

4. Attention to the demands of time, place and modern problems.

5. Complete and perfect awareness of all chapters and books of jurisprudence and even knowledge of the four schools of jurisprudence of Ahle Sunnat.

One who spends years in attending lectures and debates in the religious colleges is able to reach to the position of Ijtihad and deriving the laws of Shariah. Such a person has the capability to derive the laws of Shariah from its reliable sources.

Mujtahid, is the real knower of Islam, having full awareness of the events that have taken place in the world, which have influenced individual, social, ethical, cultural, political and economic conditions of the Muslim Ummah and who solves the problems of jurisprudence through a broad point of view and guides the Muslim Ummah for success in the world and the hereafter.

The true jurist, through his profound insight, is able to bear the responsibility of fulfilling the needs of people in every time and place. Moreover, he keeps away from deviation, harshness, wrong interpretations and innovations of the deviated. He derives legal and suitable ways and entrusts it to the government and Islamic society and through this, practically proves the perpetuality of Islam.

In traditions, such a Mujtahid is described as inheritor of prophets and outpost of defense of Islam.

Imam Ja'far Sadiq (a) said: Confusion does not frustrate one who possesses the know-how of his time.[161]

Ali bin Abi Hamza says: 'When a true believer dies, the angels and the parts of earth where he worshipped Allah, weep because of his death. Also the doors of the heavens through which his good deeds had been taken up weep and it causes an irreparable damage in the Islamic system. It is because the true believing Fuqaha[162], people of proper understanding in religion and its laws are the strongholds of the Islamic system just as the fortress around a city is a stronghold for it.'"[163]

---

[161] Al-Kafi, Vol. 1, Pg. 26

[162] Islamic jurists

[163] Al-Kafi, Vol. 1, Pg. 38

Taqlid

Taqlid implies following a jurist and taking laws of Shariah from him. A fully qualified Mujtahid is a person who has specialized in deriving the laws of Shariah. Persons who do not have this specialization have no option, except to refer to the jurist in learning their duties and laws of religion, because referring of the ignorant persons to experts is logical; like a patient consulting a doctor, a student to a teacher, farmer to the agricultural engineer etc.

Part VI: Branches of Religion (Furu Deen)

Prayer

Prayer

Prayer is the pillar of religion and the best of its worship acts. A number of times every day, Muslims leave aside worldly engagements and focus their attention to the Merciful Lord. They perform ablution and with perfect sincerity, stand before the Creator of the universe and become engrossed in ritual prayer. They have confidential conversation with their God and speak to Him directly. They connect their heart to Almighty Allah and through His remembrance, they illuminate their hearts.

This worship act is having a special importance and it is highly emphasized in verses of Quran and traditions of Prophet.

The Holy Quran says:

"And keep up prayer and pay the poor-rate and bow down

with those who bow down." (2:43)

"O you who believe! seek assistance through patience and prayer; surely Allah is with the patient." (2:153)

"Say to My servants who believe that they should keep up prayer and spend out of what We have given them secretly and openly before the coming of the day in which there shall be no bartering nor mutual befriending." (14:31)

"Recite that which has been revealed to you of the Book and keep up prayer; surely prayer keeps (one) away from indecency and evil, and certainly the remembrance of Allah is the greatest, and Allah knows what you do." (29:45)

Zaid says: I heard Imam Ja'far Sadiq (a) say: The best deed in the view of Almighty Allah is Prayer and it is also the last advice of the prophets. How nice it is that man performs the ritual bath (Ghusl) or ablution (Wudhu) and after that he stands up to pray: bowing and prostrating, while no one is looking at him. When a person prolongs his prostration, Shaitan wails: O woe, this person has obeyed God, while I disobeyed Him. He is prostrating and I refused to perform it.[164]

The Messenger of Allah (s) said: When a believer servant stands up for prayer, Almighty Allah looks at him till he concludes the prayer, divine mercy surrounds him from above his head to the heavens. Angels surround him from around him to the heavens. Allah appoints an angel on him, who says: O worshipper, if you knew who looks upon you and with whom you talk in secret, you would never finish the

---

[164] Al-Kafi, Vol. 3, Pg. 264

prayer and would not move from your place.[165]

The Messenger of Allah said: On Judgment Day, people shall be called for accounting. The first point one would be questioned about is prayer. Thus, if he had fulfilled this duty with sincerity and in proper manner, he would get salvation and if not, he would be thrown into Hellfire.[166]

In the same way, he said: One who considers Prayers unimportant is not from me. By Allah, he would not meet me at the Pool of Kauthar. And one who drinks wine is not from me. By Allah, he would not meet me at the Pool of Kauthar.[167]

Islam has not only emphasized the offering of Prayer, it has asked Muslims to establish Prayer; that is they should consider Prayer as an important duty and try for its establishment. They should be attentive to the times of Prayer. They should hasten to it at the earliest time. They should be present in Masjids and pray in congregation. They should accord priority to it over all other activities. The command of Prayer was so important in Islam that intentional omission of it, without any excuse is considered to be a greater sin even upto the extent of disbelief.

Imam Ja'far Sadiq (a) has narrated that a man came to the Messenger of Allah (s) and said: O Messenger of Allah (s), please dispense advice to me. He said: Do not omit Prayer intentionally as Muslim Ummah has declared immunity from one who omits it intentionally.[168]

Jabir has narrated that the Messenger of Allah (s) said: There is no gap between disbelief and faith, except the omitting of Prayer.[169]

---

[165] Al-Kafi, Vol. 3, Pg. 265

[166] Wasailush Shia, Vol. 4, Pg. 30

[167] Wasailush Shia, Vol. 4, Pg. 25

[168] Wasailush Shia, Vol. 4, Pg. 42

[169] Wasailush Shia, Vol. 4, Pg. 43

Presence of mind during Prayers and attention to Almighty Allah is also very important. Recitations and recitals, bowings and prostrations, Tasha-hud[170] and Salam[171] form the structure of Prayer. But presence of mind is having the position of the soul of Prayer. Soul of the worshipper, who prays with the presence of mind, rises up towards God to reach the position of proximity. Although presence of mind is not a necessary condition of correctness of Prayer, but it is the criterion of its value and acceptance; that is why it is much emphasized.

The Holy Prophet (s) said: There is difference in acceptance of prayers; in some half, one third, one fourth, one fifth till one tenth of it is accepted. And some prayers, like an old dress is twisted and thrown at the face of the worshipper. Indeed your benefit from prayer is proportionate to your sincere attention to God.[172]

He also said: One who is attentive to anything other than Allah in Prayers, Allah says to him: O My servant, in whose pursuit are you and whom do you seek? Do you seek a lord other than Me? Or do you seek the attention of someone other than Me? Or do you desire the blessings of someone other than Me? Whereas I am the most merciful, generous and reward giver; in prayer, I give you a reward, which is unlimited. Pay attention to Me, because I and My angels have focused our attention to you. Thus, if the worshipper turns his attention to Almighty Allah, his sin of the past inattention is forgiven. If the second time also, he becomes attentive to someone other than God. The Almighty repeats the same statements; thus if he returns and again focuses his attention to God, the Almighty also overlooks his past carelessness. If the third time, again he becomes attentive to someone other than God, Almighty

---

[170] A part of ritual of Prayer performed in seated position at the end of the second and the last unit.

[171] Final salutation indicating end of the Prayer.

[172] Biharul Anwar, Vol. 84, Pg. 260

Allah also repeats the same words. Thus, if the worshipper turns his attention to Almighty Allah, the Almighty forgives his previous sin. But if the fourth time again he becomes inattentive from Allah, Almighty Allah and His angels turn away from him and Almighty Allah says: O servant, I leave you to that, which you like and which you seek.[173]

Types of Prayers

Prayers can be divided into two types: Obligatory and recommended. Five kinds of prayers are obligatory:

1. Daily obligatory prayers: that is Morning, Noon, Afternoon, Evening and Night.

2. Ayaat Prayer: This is a two-unit prayer recited on special occasions in a particular manner. Ayaat Prayer becomes obligatory when there is solar or lunar eclipse, or there is earthquake or a great natural disaster takes place, which generally terrifies people.

3. Funeral Prayer: This Prayer is prayed in a particular way over the dead body of a Muslim.

4. Prayer of circumambulating (Tawaf) of an Obligatory Hajj: This is a two unit prayer and it is performed after the Tawaf of Hajj and Umrah.

5. Lapsed Prayers of the father are obligatory on the eldest son.

Recommended Prayers are numerous and most of them consist of two units each; like the Nafila[174] of Daily Prayer, which is prayed along the Daily Prayers; Nafila of Noon Prayer is eight units and it is prayed before Noon Prayer and similarly Nafila of Afternoon Prayer is also eight units and it is also prayed before Afternoon Prayer. Nafila of Evening Prayer is four units after Evening Prayer and Nafila of Night Prayer is two units after Night Prayer if performed in the sitting

---

[173] Biharul Anwar, Vol. 84, Pg. 244

[174] Extra supererogatory prayer

position; and Nafila of Morning Prayer is two units and it is prayed before Morning Prayer.

Midnight Prayer is also an emphasized recommended Nafila Prayer, which is prayed just before dawn. It consists of eight units recited in units of two prayed with intention of Shab[175] prayer; then two units with intention of Shafa[176] Prayer and then one unit with intention of Witr[177] Prayer.

Other recommended prayers are also there, which are recited on particular occasions. Those who are interested may refer to books of supplications.

Fasting

Fasting

Another important Islamic worship act is fasting. A person, who intents to fast, has to, from dawn to sunset (Maghrib), avoid all acts that invalidate fast. Fasting is a worship act and it is performed with intention of proximity of God; and any show off or ostentation invalidates it.

Numerous traditions are recorded with regard to the excellence of fasting:

The Messenger of Allah (s) said: Fasting is a shield against Hellfire.[178]

---

[175] Midnight Prayer

[176] Even

[177] Odd

[178] Al-Kafi, Vol. 4, Pg. 62

Imam Ja'far Sadiq (a) said: Almighty Allah says: Fasting is My property and I am the reward of fasting.[179]

In the same way, he said: Sleep of the person, who is fasting, is a worship act, his silence is glorification of God, his deed is accepted and his supplication is answered.[180]

The Messenger of Allah (s) said: Allah, the Mighty and Sublime says: All the good deeds are rewarded from ten to seven hundred times, except for patience, which is reserved for Me and I am its reward. Only Allah knows the reward of patience. Patience implies fasting.[181]

Imam Muhammad Baqir (a) said: Islam is based on five pillars: Prayer, Zakat, Hajj, Fasting and Wilayat.[182]

It is obligatory for every Muslim who has reached the age of maturity and who has no legal excuse, to fast in the month of Ramadhan. If he invalidates his fast without a legal excuse, he has committed a greater sin and in addition of making up for it later, he also has to pay the penalty (Kaffarah) of either (1) keeping another sixty fasts or (2) feeding sixty poor persons or (3) freeing a slave in the way of Allah.

Some people are exempt from fasting:

1. Fasting is not obligatory on a sick person for whom it is harmful.
2. A traveler whose return journey is eight or more Farsakhs.
3. A woman going through menses or post natal bleeding.
4. Fasting is not obligatory on a woman in advanced stage of pregnancy, for whom fasting is harmful or for the child she is carrying.
5. If a woman is suckling a child, whether she is the mother or a nurse, or suckles it free, and the quantity of her milk is small, and if fasting is harmful to her or to the child, it will not be obligatory on her

---

[179] Al-Kafi, Vol. 4, Pg. 63
[180] Wasailush Shia, Vol. 10, Pg. 401
[181] Wasailush Shia, Vol. 10, Pg. 404
[182] Al-Kafi, Vol. 4, Pg. 62

to fast.

These five groups of people are exempt from fasting, but after the month of Ramadhan, they must make up for the missed fasts, but no penalty or sin is applicable to them.

Although old women and men who cannot fast or it is difficult for them, they are not bound to keep fast and they are also not required to make up for them later.[183]

That which was mentioned about the excellence of fasting and problems related to it, was according to the verdict of Islamic jurisprudence, but scholars of moral science consider obligatory-ness of abstemiousness during fast to be more extensive. They say: Although the fast may be right from the jurists' point of view and it removes the responsibility, but for its acceptance, other matters should also be avoided, like avoiding all sins, They say: Fast of a person is perfect and it is accepted only if all the organs of his body have fasted; that is he has refrained his eyes, ears, tongue, hands and legs from sins. Such a fast is called as the fast of the special servants of Allah.

Higher than this fast is the fast of the special of the special servants of God; and it is that the keeper of fast in addition to abstaining from invalidating factors according to jurisprudence and committing of sins, should also restrain his mind from paying attention to anyone other than God; he should consider Almighty Allah to be really present and seeing.

Muhammad bin Ijlan says: I heard Imam Ja'far Sadiq (a) say: Fasting is not only refraining from eating and drinking; on the contrary when you fast, your ears and eyes, tongue and stomach and private parts should also be fasting. You should be mindful of your hands and private

---

[183] In addition to the fasts of Ramadhan, there are other obligatory fasts also; in the same way, there a large number of recommended fasts; unlawful and detestable fasts are also there whose details are given in books of Islamic code of law.

parts; you should be quiet, except for a good word and during the period of fasting, be moderate to your servant.[184]

Imam Ja'far Sadiq (a) said: When you are fasting, keep your ears and eyes aloof from prohibited and evil acts. Avoid useless arguments and torture of servants. Dignity of the fast should be obvious on you. The day you are fasting should not be like the day you are not.[185]

The Messenger of Allah (s) said: One who fasts in silence during the month of Ramadhan and protects his ears, eyes, tongue, private parts and limbs with intention of divine proximity, Almighty Allah makes him near to Himself, in such a way that his feet touch the footsteps of Ibrahim, the Friend of Allah (Khalilullah).[186]

One who is fasting is invited to the feast of Almighty Lord and he should observe the manners of social interaction and should not commit a misdemeanor. He should try to be a real keeper of fast so that he may benefit his balance of deeds with divine blessing and rewards, which are more exalted and more valuable than material rewards.

Imam Ja'far Sadiq (a) said: The keeper of fast roams in the gardens of Paradise and enjoys them. Angels pray for him till he ends the fast (Iftar).[187]

Amirul Momineen (a) has narrated from the Holy Prophet (s) that he asked the Almighty Allah on the Night of Ascension (Meraj): My Lord, which is the foremost worship act? He replied: Fasting. He asked: What is the reward of fasting? He replied: Fasting is followed by wisdom and wisdom causes divine recognition and recognition causes certainty. When a person becomes a person of certainty, it does not

---

[184] Wasailush Shia, Vol. 10, Pg. 165

[185] Wasailush Shia, Vol. 10, Pg. 163

[186] Wasailush Shia, Vol. 10, Pg. 164

[187] Wasailush Shia, Vol. 10, Pg. 406

make any difference whether he is in hardship or ease.[188]

Hasan bin Sadaqah has narrated from Imam Musa bin Ja'far (a) that he said: Sleep for half the day, because Almighty Allah feeds a keeper of fast with food and water when he is sleeping.[189]

Amirul Momineen (a) said: One day the Messenger of Allah (s) delivered a sermon to us and said: O people, the month of Allah is coming to you with blessings and forgiveness. It is the best month in the view of God. Its days are the best days and its nights are the best of nights; and its hours are the best hours. In this best month, you are the guest of Almighty Allah and are recipients of His blessings and kindness. Your breathing is having the reward of divine glorification. Your sleep is considered as worship; your deeds are accepted and your supplications are fulfilled.[190]

Philosophy of Fasting

Fasting is one of the best ways of purification and discipline of the self and wayfaring on way to Allah. If it is performed according divine commands, it removes the rust of carelessness and sins from the heart and makes it clean and illuminated. It removes the satans from the abode of the heart and prepares it for the arrival of angels and brilliance of light, wisdom and certainty. Such fasting is acceptance of invitation of God Almighty and makes one eligible to obtain divine rewards. Without any doubt he would also get favors of the merciful Lord.

The second philosophy of fasting is that rich people who keep fasts experience the hunger usually experienced by the poor and become concerned about those who are mostly facing food shortages and motivate them to render help to them.

Hisham bin Hakam asked Imam Ja'far Sadiq (a) about the philosophy

---

[188] Biharul Anwar, Vol. 77, Pg. 27

[189] Al-Kafi, Vol. 4, Pg. 65

[190] Wasailush Shia, Vol. 10, Pg. 313

of fasting. Imam (a) said: Allah has deemed fasting as obligatory so that the rich and poor become equal, because the wealthy do not at all experience hunger, except in Ramadhan, so that they might be considerate to the poor and Allah desired that they should taste the bitterness of hunger during days of fasting and be considerate to the hungry.[191]

Imam Ali Reza (a) wrote in reply to the question to Muhammad bin Sinan: The reason why fasting is obligatory is that the keeper of fast may experience hunger and thirst, till he faces hardship and indigence and becomes rewarded and patient and that it be a testimony of the hardships of the hereafter, and it be means of suppression of selfish desires, a kind of moral lesson and guidance of the hereafter, so that he may understand the meaning of poverty and depravity of the world and the hereafter.[192]

With the help of the above philosophy of fasting, it is possible to help in solving the problem of hunger in the world to some extent. That is, since the keepers of fasts who live in the world abstain from food on the prescribed days, they save the amount of food and at the end of the month they give that accumulated quantity to the needy persons of their society or country; it would be substantial help of poor. Now if the taxes and charities, which are recommended and emphasized, are added up, it would reach a considerable figure for the poor and hungry. Although it is subject to the condition that it should be in accordance to a proper plan of collection and should be spent in the right way.

The third and the most important philosophy of fasting is discipline of self and inculcating in oneself the habit of avoiding sins and gaining piety. During the month of Ramadhan, the sincere keepers of fasts keep away from sins with absolute determination. On the contrary,

---

[191] Wafi, Vol. 11, Pg. 33

[192] Wafi, Vol. 11, Pg. 34

they even avoid lawful pleasures like eating and drinking etc. Or with the intention of proximity they continue this physical and spiritual discipline for a month. Such persons develop such strength and determination that even after this month they can remain on piety. The Holy Quran has also hinted this point when it says:

> "*O you who believe! fasting is prescribed for you, as it was prescribed for those before you, so that you may guard (against evil)." (2:183)*

Hajj

Hajj

Hajj in Islam is one of the great worship acts and is considered as a pillar of Islam. Imam Muhammad Baqir (a) said: Islam is based on five pillars: Prayer, Zakat, Hajj, Fasting and Wilayat.

Hajj should be performed with intention of seeking divine proximity; show off and ostentation leads to its invalidation. Rituals of Hajj are performed in the special days of the month of Zilhajj and it is obligatory once in a lifetime on every Muslim who has the capability and means of travel.

Hajj is a great and comprehensive worship act and its legislation has many aims. And if it is performed in the proper manner, it carries important advantages for the pilgrim as well as the great Muslim community. Therefore, Prophet Ibrahim (a) was appointed by Almighty Allah to call people to it.

The Holy Quran says:

> "And proclaim among men the Pilgrimage: they will come to you on foot and on every lean camel, coming from every remote path. That they may witness advantages for them and mention the name of Allah during stated days over what He has given them of the cattle quadrupeds, then eat of them and feed the distressed one, the needy." (22:27-28)

Attention to Allah and discipline of the self

One of the important advantages and aims of Hajj is purification, discipline, development of self and gaining proximity to Allah. Hajj is a spiritual and ideal journey, in which the Hajj pilgrim prepares himself before setting out to visit the House of God and to be there in the presence of the Lord. He repents for his past sins, which cause distancing from Almighty Allah. He repays his debts, purifies his wealth from unlawful and obligatory rights and if he has oppressed anyone, he obtains his forgiveness.

At that time, he sets out towards the House of God and throughout the journey, he considers himself to be the guest of Allah, who is in His presence and always having His remembrance. He performs these rituals with insight and with attention to their wisdoms. When in Miqaat (starting point) he puts on two pieces of white cloth, without any stain and becomes a Muhrim (one who is dressed in pilgrim garb), he also purifies his inner being from sins and worldly relations. He chants the Thalbiya (slogan of: Here I am, My Lord) as acceptance of the invitation of Almighty Allah and throughout his period of Ihram, he does nothing, which is against its decorum.

In this condition, he moves towards the House of God. As much one is sincere, as much his heart is proximate to Allah. While circumambulating the Kaaba, during Tawaf Prayer, Sayy (trotting) between Safa and Marwah etc. he is consistently having remembrance of Allah.

By halting in Arafat, one is reminded of the halting on Judgment Day and during the process of accounting of deeds. In Mina and halt in Mashar, he sees himself to be in the condition of moving towards Almighty Allah. During the stoning of satans, he also stones his baser self (Nafse Ammara) and the satans; at the time of slaughtering the sheep in the slaughtering area, he is reminded of the ranks of obedience and loyalty of Prophet Ibrahim and Ismail (a) and he fulfills all the rituals of Hajj in this condition. In the end, he makes a firm determination that he would never again commit sinful acts and that he would always protect the sanctity and value of being a Haji. At that time, with illuminated self, confident heart, a satisfied mind and an absolute determination and an accepted Hajj he returns to his hometown.

This advantage is considered to be the most important benefits of Hajj and it is also hinted at in traditions:

Imam Ja'far Sadiq (a) said: Hajj and Umrah are two markets of the markets of the hereafter. One, who goes for Hajj and Umrah, is in the neighborhood of divine mercy. If he gets the good sense (Taufeeq) to complete the rituals of Hajj, his sins are forgiven and if his death occurs, his reward is on Almighty Allah.[193]

In the same way, he said: When people camp at Mina, a caller from Almighty Allah calls out: If you knew in whose neighborhood you are situated, you would be certain that Allah, the Mighty and the High is your successor in protecting your wealth and family and He blesses you with His forgiveness.[194]

He also said: When you decide to perform the Hajj, make your mind

---

[193] Al-Kafi, Vol. 14, Pg. 240

[194] Al-Kafi, Vol. 14, Pg. 263

Part VI: Branches of Religion (Furu Deen)

free of every apprehension and obstruction for Almighty Allah; leave your affairs on Allah; and in all actions rely on God and be content with His will and decree. Leave the world and it contents for the people and fulfill the rights that others have on you. Do not rely on your provisions, conveyance, companions, youth and wealth, lest all of them create problems for you, because one who is seeking the pleasure of Allah, but relies on anything other than Him, Allah makes that same thing as a means of trouble for him. You should prepare for the journey of Hajj in such a way as if you have no hope of return. Be congenial with your companions; observe with diligence the times of obligatory divine duties and recommended practices (Sunnah) of the Prophet. Always be observant of Islamic manners, bearing hardships, patience, thankfulness, kindness, charity and loyalty. At that time, wash your sins with the pure water of repentance, put on a proper and clean dress of sincerity and become aloof (Muhrim) from everything, which prevents you from the remembrance and obedience of Allah. At that moment, with a true and sincere slogan of 'Here I am, my Lord' (Labbaik) reply to the call of truth and attach yourself to the firm rope of God. Like you circle the House of God with other Muslims, with a sincere heart in the company of angels circle the empyrean. In Harwala[195] abstain from following your selfish desires.

When you set out from Arafat to Mina, declare immunity from your power and become free of carelessness and mistakes and do not aspire for that, which is not lawful for you and which you have no right of.

In Arafat confess to your mistakes and renew with Almighty Allah your covenant about belief in His oneness. In Muzdalifah, seek proximity to Almighty Allah and adopt piety and fear of God. When you climb the mountain, take along your soul to a higher level as well.

At the time of sacrifice, cut off the throat of selfish desires and greed.

---

[195] Peculiar pace of Hajj pilgrims.

When you stone the Satans stone the base desires and bad morals. By shaving the head, remove your hidden and apparent defects as well.

When you enter the holy sanctuary, consider yourself in the refuge of God for the fulfillment of your wishes. And prepare yourself to pay respect to the owner of the House and recognition of His majesty and Power. During circumambulation (Tawaf) kiss the Black Stone with satisfaction and contentment. In the farewell circumambulation, forsake anything other than God. When you halt on Mount Safa, purify your inner soul for meeting Allah. When you climb Mount Marwah, repose yourself with piety to the presence of God and till Judgment Day remain faithful to the promises and covenants you have made to Him. Know that Almighty Allah has not made Hajj obligatory and among all worship acts has not related it to Himself and has not accorded importance to prophets in proper sequence in the rituals of Hajj, except that by witnessing the ritual of Hajj by sane persons, they should prepare themselves and get instruction for death and grave, the resurrection and Judgment Day, separation of the righteous from the evil doers and entry of the dwellers of Paradise into Paradise and the dwellers of Hell into Hellfire.[196]

The Messenger of Allah (s) said: The sign that Hajj is accepted is that when the pilgrim returns to his hometown, he never commits any sins. If after returning, he again commits sins like adultery, cheating or other sins, it would be known that his Hajj has not been accepted.[197]

The Holy Prophet (s) said in the sermon of Ghadeer: O people, perform the Hajj and visit the holy places associated with it with perfection of faith and recognition of its correct method and do not turn away from the holy places, except after you have repented for

---

[196] Mustadrakul Wasail, Vol. 10, Pg. 172

[197] Mustadrakul Wasail, Vol. 10, Pg. 165

your sins.[198]

Universal gathering of Muslim Ummah

The second benefit of Hajj is participation of the Muslim Ummah in a social gathering. Gathering of Hajj is a great conference of the Islamic world, which is held in Mecca every year and in the vicinity of sanctuary of Almighty Allah. Some Muslims from every country participate in it and through it become aware of political, social, cultural, economic difficulties of each other. They cooperate with each other in solving problems and in exchanging views; and with morals and manners, become aware of each other from close quarters.

Previously it was mentioned that Islam considers all Muslims to be a single community having common interests and responsibilities, which are as follows:

1. Propagation and original culture of Islam among itself and in other communities.

2. Confrontation with polytheism, idols and false deities, who have trespassed on the sanctities of the oneness of Godhead and considered themselves to be having the right to legislate laws and administering the Islamic countries.

3. Endeavoring to strengthen the unity of Islamic countries and sects.

4. Protecting the independence of the great nation of Islam.

5. Confronting the domination of enemies in Islamic countries.

6. Defending Islamic territories.

7. Defending Islam and confronting the powers opposed to Islam.

8. Defense of the rights of the Muslims of the world.

9. Confronting the invasion of debased culture and corrupted morals of the enemies of Islam.

---

[198] Mustadrakul Wasail, Vol. 10, Pg. 174

10. Guidance of the young generation.
11. Defending the rights of women.
12. Defending the rights of children.
13. Defending the rights of the deprived and poor.
14. Defending the victims and the oppressed.

And other important matters, which are related to the Muslim world.

Muslim Ummah can assume the form of a single community, which is independent and powerful; having self respect in the world and is able to defend its reality; which is united and in defense of unity and fulfillment of common responsibilities it should be concerned and proactive. Although the fulfillment of this living and important matter also is not possible without the existence of an integrated and powerful movement.

On the basis of this, formation of a public gathering for the Muslim world is necessary; a gathering which is attended by Muslims from every country and Muslim sect and that they exchange views and suggestions in important matters related to the world of Islam. Representatives of the world of Islamic countries throughout the years have participated in public gatherings and commissions and discussed the important problems of the Muslim world and this matter can best be achieved through the gathering of Hajj.

Although such an extensive organization is needed for the Muslim world, which venue can be more suitable for it than the sanctuary of God and the neighborhood of monotheism?

The Holy Quran says:

> **"Most surely the first house appointed for men is the one at Mecca, blessed and (a) guidance for the nations. In it are clear signs, the standing place of Ibrahim, and whoever enters it shall be secure, and pilgrimage to the House is**

Part VI. Branches of Religion (Furu Deen)

incumbent upon men for the sake of Allah, (upon) every one who is able to undertake the journey to it; and whoever disbelieves, then surely Allah is Self-sufficient, above any need of the worlds." (3:96-97)

It also says:

"And when We made the House a pilgrimage for men and a (place of) security, and: Appoint for yourselves a place of prayer on the standing-place of Ibrahim. And We enjoined Ibrahim and Ismail saying: Purify My House for those who visit (it) and those who abide (in it) for devotion and those who bow down (and) those who prostrate themselves." (2:125)

In the same way, it says:

"Allah has made the Kaaba, the sacred house, a maintenance for the people, and the sacred month and the offerings and the sacrificial animals with garlands; this is that you may know that Allah knows whatever is in the heavens and whatever is in the earth, and that Allah is the Knower of all things." (5:97)

In the above verses, Kaaba is introduced as 'blessed', 'guidance for the nations', 'a (place of) security', 'a maintenance for the people'; thus it is known that the Holy Kaaba is the most suitable and the best venue of a public gathering on the Muslim world, and independence and greatness of Muslim Ummah is related to it. Therefore, it is necessary for it to be a source of blessing, bounty and guidance for the Muslim world.

Establishment of such an organization is from the greatest advantages of Hajj. If people of foresight and well wishers of Muslims had established this important organization the circumstances of the Muslim Ummah would definitely have been better; but regretfully such an organization does not exist and its establishment is very difficult in such conditions. In any case, international Islamic organizations can be established on the basis of views of the enlightened and well wishers of the world of Islam and its need should be justified and it should be propagated in the form of a single Islamic view and the background should be prepared for its establishment.

In the same way, Mecca should be deemed as the permanent venue of organization of conference of Muslim countries and it should be endeavored that they should also try to be concerned and proactive in the issues related to the Muslim world.

In the present circumstances, advantage can be taken from the rituals of Hajj and conferences can be held on different subjects in Mecca and Medina. If these conferences follow a detailed program, with awareness of authorities of the hosting country, they would definitely help in creating general awareness about Muslims.

Display of Unity

The third benefit of Hajj is general participation of all Muslims in rituals and renewal of oath of unity and display of power before infidelity and world imperialism. Islam is a religion of monotheism. The most important aim of the Prophet of Islam (s) was confrontation with polytheism and false deities. He was appointed from the side of Almighty Allah so that he may wave the standard of monotheism in the world to completely eradicate idol worship and polytheism. The Messenger of Allah (s) accepted this great responsibility without any worry or fear and openly expressed immunity from polytheism and polytheists. He also ordered Ali Ibne Abi Talib (a) to recite the verses of Surah Baraat in the crowd of Hajj pilgrims to the House of Allah. As the Holy Quran says:

"And an announcement from Allah and His Apostle to the people on the day of the greater pilgrimage that Allah and His Apostle are free from liability to the idolaters; therefore if you repent, it will be better for you, and if you turn back, then know that you will not weaken Allah; and announce painful punishment to those who disbelieve." (9:3)

By the recitation of Surah Baraat in the crowd of Muslims, the Holy Prophet (s) declared immunity from polytheism, polytheists, false deities and idol worshippers and declared confrontation against them and brought it out in the form of a customary program of Muslims.

After the passing away of the Holy Prophet (s), this responsibility came upon the Muslims. They are duty bound to completely fulfill the objectives of the Prophet and they must not forsake the standard of defending monotheism and confronting infidelity and hegemony.

Have the aims and aspirations of the great Prophet of Islam fulfilled so that Muslims may now take rest and remain quiet? Are the majority of the people in the world still not idolaters? Are tyrants and oppressors still not dominating the people? Have all the deprived people of the world been able to have their legal rights restored? Has Islam emerged victorious over infidelity and hegemony? Has Palestine been liberated from Zionism and all conspiracies to eradicate Islam have been destroyed? And hundreds of other question!!

On the basis of this, Muslims should continue to declare immunity from the idolaters and should defend monotheism in every way. In order to fulfill this religious obligation, no better place exists than the sanctuary of God, which is the original outpost of monotheism and within a crowd of world Muslims and pilgrims who come to perform Hajj of the House of God.[199]

Holy Struggle (Jihad)

Holy Struggle (Jihad)

Jihad, according to its literary meaning, is struggle and bearing of difficulties on the path of an aim. In terminology also, it implies extreme efforts in battle in order to spread Islam and propagation of the word of monotheism or defense of Islam and Muslims.

Jihad is one of the important Islamic duties, which is having a special rank, because spread, survival, power, greatness and independence of Islam and application of religious laws are all based on this matter only. Therefore, there is great emphasis regarding it in Quran and traditions.

The Holy Quran says:

"Do you think that you will enter the garden while Allah has not yet known those who strive hard from among you, and (He has not) known the patient." (3:142)

"O Prophet! Strive hard against the unbelievers and the hypocrites and be unyielding to them; and their abode is hell,

---

[199] Hajj is a worship act, whose rituals are performed in a particular way in a particular time period. The method of this worship act and their commands and prohibitions require details and explanations, which regrettably is not possible here. Those who are interested may refer to books of Islamic jurisprudence.

and evil is the destination." (9:73)

"Fighting is enjoined on you, and it is an object of dislike to you; and it may be that you dislike a thing while it is good for you, and it may be that you love a thing while it is evil for you, and Allah knows, while you do not know." (2:216)

"The holders back from among the believers, not having any injury, and those who strive hard in Allah's way with their property and their persons are not equal; Allah has made the strivers with their property and their persons to excel the holders back a (high) degree, and to each (class) Allah has promised good; and Allah shall grant to the strivers above the holders back a mighty reward." (4:95)

"Surely Allah loves those who fight in His way in ranks as if they were a firm and compact wall." (61:4)

Amirul Momineen (a) said: Jihad is a gate from the gates of Paradise, which Almighty Allah has opened for His special friends and has prepared them for Paradise, so that they may earn the nobility from Allah and the bounties that He has reserved for them. Jihad is a garment of piety, a firm armor of God and shield against the attack of enemies. One, who becomes aloof from Jihad; Almighty Allah dresses him in the dress of degradation, calamities surround him and he becomes distanced from the pleasure of God; he meets extreme humiliation and degradation and the veil of his heart is removed. By omitting Jihad, the wealth of truth is taken away from him, and he is involved in debasements and hardships and he is deprived from justice and equity.[200]

The Messenger of Allah (s) said: There is a gate of Paradise, which named as 'Gate of the holy fighters'. The holy fighters with sword fixed to their waists and people would be halted at the stop on Judgment Day and angels would be welcoming them. They would move to Paradise and its gates would open for them. [Then he said:] One who omits Jihad, Allah, the Mighty and Sublime humiliates him and makes him poor and his religion suffers a loss, because Allah, the Mighty and the High would make my Ummah needless of the hooves of the horses and centers of power.[201]

Amirul Momineen (a) said: Allah, the Mighty and the High made Jihad obligatory and mentioned it with praise and mentioned it to be a means of success and rendering help to Him. By Allah, religion and the world of the people are not reformed, except through Jihad.[202] Jihad is divided into two kinds: Offensive and defensive.

Offensive Jihad

The Messenger of Allah (s) was sent from Almighty Allah in order to confront injustice and polytheism and he called people to the religion of Islam.

And that he may set free the deprived and poor from the domination of oppressors and tyrants. The Messenger of Allah (s) in the beginning called the people through a pleasing way of speaking and through logical reasonings to accept Islam and to eschew infidelity and idol worship. If hurdles had not appeared in his path, he would have continued this same style till the final victory, but leaders of polytheism and infidelity and the arrogant and oppressors perceived danger from

---

[200] Al-Kafi, Vol. 5, Pg. 4

[201] Al-Kafi, Vol. 5, Pg. 2

[202] Al-Kafi, Vol. 5, Pg. 8

this call and they began to devise plots and create hurdles against him. Therefore, they used all means in order to assure that Islam does not spread or become dominant.

In such circumstances and conditions, the Prophet and Muslims had no option, except to make war and perform Jihad in order to achieve their aims. They performed Jihad in order to show to the oppressors and tyrants their place, removed their obstructions and prepared the atmosphere for propagation and spread of Islam.

In this way, it can be said: Offensive Jihad is also a kind of defense. The Holy Quran says:

> "And if they break their oaths after their agreement and (openly) revile your religion, then fight the leaders of unbelief - surely their oaths are nothing - so that they may desist. What! will you not fight a people who broke their oaths and aimed at the expulsion of the Apostle, and they attacked you first; do you fear them? But Allah is most deserving that you should fear Him, if you are believers." (9:12-13)

> "And fight with them until there is no persecution, and religion should be only for Allah, but if they desist, then there should be no hostility except against the oppressors." (2:193)

Defensive Jihad

Defensive Jihad is also performed for defense of Islam and Muslim countries. This Jihad becomes obligatory in a few instances:

1. In case when enemies of Islam attack the country with an aim to overthrow the Islamic government or to enact a dangerous conspiracy. The Holy Quran says:

"And fight in the way of Allah with those who fight with you, and do not exceed the limits, surely Allah does not love those who exceed the limits." (2:190)

2. When the enemies of Islam launch an attack on a Muslim country in order to extend their territories and to obtain hegemony over Islamic lands.

"Permission (to fight) is given to those upon whom war is made, because they are oppressed, and most surely Allah is well able to assist them. Those who have been expelled from their homes without a just cause except that they say: Our Lord is Allah." (22:39-40)

3. When one of the Muslim countries trespasses against other Islamic countries, in addition to the fact that the attacked country is having right to defense, other Muslims as well are duty bound to support the attacked country and make peace between them and if the attacker does not refrain from fighting, they should make war against it.

The Holy Quran says:

"And if two parties of the believers quarrel, make peace between them; but if one of them acts wrongfully towards

Part VI: Branches of Religion (Furu Deen)

> *the other, fight that which acts wrongfully until it returns to Allah's command; then if it returns, make peace between them with justice and act equitably; surely Allah loves those who act equitably." (49:9)*

4. When public property of a Muslim country is attacked by the enemy.
5. When the life and honor of Muslims is a target of attack.
6. When worship of God, Mosques and worship houses are targeted by the enemies.

Quran says:

> *"And had there not been Allah's repelling some people by others, certainly there would have been pulled down cloisters and churches and synagogues and mosques in which Allah's name is much remembered; and surely Allah will help him who helps His cause; most surely Allah is Strong, Mighty." (22:40)*

7. Defense of the rights of the deprived and poor who are victims of the oppression of tyrants and have no strength to defend themselves.

Quran says:

> *"And what reason have you that you should not fight in the way of Allah and of the weak among the men and the women and the children, (of) those who say: Our Lord! cause us to go forth from this town, whose people are oppressors, and give us from Thee a guardian and give us from Thee a helper."*

(4:75)

8. Defense of Islamic ethics and culture and preventing the entry of un-Islamic culture into it.

In this matter, it is the natural right of Muslims that they should defend their religion, respect, honor, independence, Islamic territories, lives, women and children and wealth. Not only they have a right to it, on the contrary Islam has deemed it as their duty. If they are lacking in that, they would be involved in degradation in this world and in the hereafter also, they would be chastised.

The Holy Quran says:

> *"Say: If your fathers and your sons and your brethren and your mates and your kinsfolk and property which you have acquired, and the slackness of trade, which you fear and dwellings, which you like, are dearer to you than Allah and His Apostle and striving in His way, then wait till Allah brings about His command: and Allah does not guide the transgressing people." (9:24)*

Defensive Jihad in the way of God is an absolute and valuable duty of Islam as the greatness and independence of Muslims is related to it. As long as Muslims act on this duty, they have respect and power, but when the logic of Jihad and defense in the path of truth is removed from the culture of Muslims, they gradually lose their power and glory and oppressors and enemies gain dominance on them. Regretful and shameful circumstances of Muslim countries are consequences of leaving this duty unfulfilled. In order to solve these problems, we have no other option, except revival of the culture of Jihad and martyrdom.

Enjoining Good and Forbidding Evil

Enjoining Good and Forbidding Evil

Enjoining Good means to ask others to perform good deeds and Forbidding Evil means to restrain others from inappropriate or evil acts. 'Enjoining Good and Forbidding Evil' is one of the most important obligatory duties in Islam. Fulfillment of some obligatory acts and avoiding many of the prohibited acts is done through the performance of this duty. Therefore, it is highly emphasized in verses and traditions:

"And from among you there should be a party who invite to good and enjoin what is right and forbid the wrong, and these it is that shall be successful." (3:104)

"O my son! keep up prayer and enjoin the good and forbid the evil, and bear patiently that which befalls you; surely these acts require courage." (31:17)

"You are the best of the nations raised up for (the benefit of) men; you enjoin what is right and forbid the wrong and believe in Allah..." (3:110)

Muhammad bin Umar says: I heard Imam Ali Reza (a) say: It is necessary for you to enjoin good and forbid evil, otherwise evil and mischievous people would gain dominance over you, at that time when the righteous supplicate, their supplications will not be effective.[203]

Muhammad bin Arafa says: I heard Imam Ali Reza (a) say quoting from the Messenger of Allah (s) that he said: When my Ummah gives up the duty of 'Enjoining Good and Forbidding Evil', you should expect occurrence of terrible tragedies.[204]

Huzaifah has narrated that the Holy Prophet (s) said: By the one in whose hands my life is, you must enjoin good and forbid evil; if not, Almighty Allah would send a chastisement on you in such a way that if anyone of you calls Almighty Allah, your supplication will not be accepted.[205]

Abu Saeed Khudri has narrated from the Holy Prophet (s) that he said: The greatest Jihad is a true statement, which is made in the presence of a tyrant ruler.[206]

Jabir has narrated from Imam Muhammad Baqir (a) that he said: In the last period of time, a group of ostentatious people would appear. They would be engrossed in recitation of Quran, piety and worship acts, but would be ignorant and foolish. They will not consider 'Enjoining Good and Forbidding Evil' as obligatory, except when it may save them from harm. They would make excuses for its avoidance. They will emulate the mistakes of scholar and their bad character. They will perform prayers and fasting and all those acts, which do not harm their life and property. Since even prayer is harmful to their property and bodies, they give it up that as well; like they have given up the highest and the noblest of the obligations.

'Enjoining Good and Forbidding Evil' is a great Islamic duty as all other obligatory duties are fulfilled through it. When they omit

---

[203] Al-Kafi, Vol. 5, Pg. 56

[204] Al-Kafi, Vol. 5, Pg. 59

[205] Jamius Sahih, Vol. 4, Pg. 468

[206] Jamius Sahih, Vol. 4, Pg. 471

'Enjoining Good and Forbidding Evil', they become eligible for divine chastisement and the punishment befalls them. Thus, the righteous in the house of evil doers and children in the house of the aged would be destroyed. 'Enjoining Good and Forbidding Evil' is the practice of the prophets and style of the righteous. It is a great duty as all obligatory duties are fulfilled through it and become the means of peace and lawful earnings. Oppressions would come back to their perpetrators. The earth would be inhabited and revenge would be taken from the enemies and matters would become firm.

Thus, you must hate evil from your heart and perform 'Enjoining Good and Forbidding Evil' from your tongue; humiliate the evil-doers and do not at all fear criticism in the path of God. If they take lesson from it and refer to rightfulness, no harm would come to them, because 'Enjoining Good and Forbidding Evil' is only about those who oppress people and who create mischief in the land and they would be given a painful chastisement. Perform Jihad against them and hate them from the depth of your heart. Your aim in this act should be to gain the pleasure of Allah and not to get hegemony, acquire wealth and to oppress others. Continue your Jihad till they submit to the truth and be obedient to Almighty Allah.[207]

On the basis of this, it is known that 'Enjoining Good and Forbidding Evil' are important Islamic duties and responsibilities and Islam has greatly emphasized performance of this duty. And this matter is supposed to be a distinctive quality of the Islamic Ummah, because Muslims, in addition of being watchful of their selves also avoid being besmeared by others.

In any case, Muslims are duty bound to be vigilant for each other, they should urge each other to perform good deeds and to refrain from evil deeds. If this mutual vigilance is observed in the right way, it

---

[207] Al-Kafi, Vol. 5, Pg. 55

would make Muslim society safe from being imbued with oppression and moral corruption and will be guided to perfection and moral excellence.

The Holy Quran says:

> *"And (as for) the believing men and the believing women, they are guardians of each other; they enjoin good and forbid evil..." (9:71)*

On the basis of this, all should make efforts to strengthen faith, to promote recognition of duties, promoting Islamic values, acting on individual and social duties, development of religious culture, prevention of moral and social corruption and absence of trespassing on the rights of other and create the best and the righteous communities in the world, so that they be exemplars and models for others.

Islam, in addition to this, has made Muslims duty bound to be the medium nation and it has also urged the other people of the world to perform good deeds and refrained them from evil deeds. It has confronted against polytheism, infidelity and materialism and invited the people of the world to monotheism and observance of social justice.

The Holy Quran says:

> *"He it is Who sent His Apostle with guidance and the religion of truth, that He might cause it to prevail over all religions, though the polytheists may be averse." (9:33)*

"Those who, should We establish them in the land, will keep up prayer and pay the poor-rate and enjoin good and forbid evil; and Allah's is the end of affairs." (22:41)

"And thus We have made you a medium (just) nation that you may be the bearers of witness to the people and (that) the Apostle may be a bearer of witness to you..." (2:143)

On the basis of this, guidance and instruction of the people of the world is a great and sensitive responsibility, whose performance requires complete preparation and necessary prefaces, some of which are hinted below:

1. Accurate and complete identification of good and bad deeds.
2. Full awareness of the political, economic, social, religious, moral circumstances of the people of the world.
3. Sufficient awareness of religions, schools of thought and their manners, customs and beliefs.
4. Preparing and using strong modes of communication to lead and guide the people of the world in different languages.
5. Publication of newspapers and academic religious magazines in different world languages.
6. Compilation and translation of necessary and appropriate books and their extensive distribution in the world.
7. Nurturing the missionaries who are conversant with Islam and different languages and sending them to the countries of the world.
8. Establishment of a center and formation of a powerful organization for propagation of Islamic culture in the world with a large budget and extensive and widespread possibilities.

Ranks of Enjoining Good and Forbidding Evil

Enjoining Good and Forbidding Evil is performed in some stages and in some ways:

First stage: Denial and detestability of an evil in one mind. When a Muslim sees a person committing an evil act, he should be restless of this deed in his own mind and he should express his hatred to it, because it is possible that he may give up that act and would not need other stages.

Second stage: Enjoining Good and Forbidding Evil through the tongue. In this stage, he orders the opponent to perform a good act or to avoid evil deeds. In the initial stage, he should use a pleasing and kind mannerism and if it is not effective, it should be through a stern and concerned tone and if that is also of no use, it should be through scolding and reproach and if that is also not effective, through rudeness and threats.

Third stage: Through use of force and strength. The last stage of 'Enjoining Good and Forbidding Evil' is physical restraint, which in the end is joined to scolding and rudeness and that is also having weak, medium and severe stages, although it is subject to the condition that rights should not be trespassed.

Aim of 'Enjoining Good and Forbidding Evil' is to restore to health and to purify the society in every possible way.

Although for 'Enjoining Good and Forbidding Evil' one can make use of severe and tough punishments also, like application of Islamic penalties, blood monies and punishments etc. But these stages are only within the ambit of judicial machinery and administrative powers of the Islamic government.[208]

Circumstances of Muslims of the world and our responsibilities

In spite of the fact that the Muslim population of the world exceeds one billion and they live in the most sensitive areas of the world from

---

[208] For more details refer to books of jurisprudence.

Part VI: Branches of Religion (Furu Deen)

the aspect of natural resources and manpower and were owners of culture and civilization and for centuries ruled the world in a powerful and glorious way and borne the standard of knowledge and culture, but regretfully, they gradually lost their power and capability and reached this present sad condition. Below we hint at their tragic circumstances:

In spite of the fact that Islam considers all Muslims of the world as a single community, regrettably under the influence of ignorance and foolishness communal and racial bias, selfishness, conspiracies and discord created by the enemies, it has been divided into small and big countries in such way that they have no unity and cooperation between them.

In these disunited countries Islam is not dominant; on the contrary, the ruler of every country has handed over the administrative powers to irreligious powers and enemies of Islam and Muslims.

Powerful countries of infidelity and hegemony have overpowered Muslim countries and seized control on all their matters.

They even interfere in their problems like selection of political, economic, academics and industry, lawmaking, agriculture and animal husbandry, arts and crafts, defense and even in religious affairs and have them under their control as well.

They take over their natural resources at paltry cost and in return give in return useless commodities and unnecessary luxury items and use those countries as markets for their goods.

They make Islamic countries suspicious of each other and create discord among them, not long ago they pitied one country against the other so that it may seek assistance from them to procure weapons and that it may accept their conditions and become their protectorate. At that time, they pose themselves to be their best supporters. They design their defense bases, sign common defense treaties and hold joint military exercises.

Regretfully, most Muslim countries are involved in these hardships and directly or indirectly live as vassals of one of the oppressive and infidel countries and sometimes they are pleased of these circumstances and feel proud of it.

On the other hand, Muslim countries are indifferent to each other; there are no friendly and cooperative relations among them and they do not trust each other. Instead of trusting each other, they rely on enemies of Islam and sign pacts of friendship and cooperation with them.

In most Muslim countries, the rulers themselves put up the regime for sale, which is not only not in defense of Islam and values of Islam, on the contrary it suppresses Islamic movements with all strength and with such a strong hand as if it is ruled over by cruel infidels and idolaters.

It was due to conspiracies hatched by the enemies of Islam and indifference of Islamic countries that the Holy land of Palestine and Masjid Aqsa was seized from Muslims by the Zionist traitors and ten years have passed and the usurpers are still ruling over it. With extensive help of infidel and hegemonic soldiers they are equipped with advanced weaponry and their military base has developed into the largest base and has posed threat to the Muslim world. International hegemony is also defending its existence with all its power.

One of the best evidence of enmity and hatred of international hegemony towards Muslims are the furious attacks of America on Muslim countries and slaying of innocent people and the destruction of their homes, whereas it considers itself to be at the forefront in confronting terrorism.

Is this civilization and defense of human rights?!

Another example of enmity of infidelity and tyranny with Islam and Muslims and aggression against religion is attack on the Muslim countries of Afghanistan and Iraq, which is still in progress and hundreds of thousands have been killed.

Emphasis of the West to spread debased culture and immoralities in Islamic countries and spending enormous budgets in this regard and instigation and support to writers, who are opposed to Islam to write and publish books against Islam; defending them under the pretext of freedom of speech and defense of human rights etc. are all a part of a well designed conspiracy to wipe off Islam.

In any case, the enemies of religion, started their enmity to Islam and Muslims from the time of the Prophet of Islam (s) and it continues to this day, in such a way that in the present age, it has become more consistent and severe and they have with all their strength, risen up to battle against Islam and Muslims. So much so, that in order to achieve their objectives they employ instruments of politics, economy, culture, arts, academics, military, rights, crimes and destroying generations, because they are faced with awakening and movements among Muslims and they perceive danger.

Insufficient and regrettable circumstances and conditions of the Muslim world, pains the heart of every liberal person and it causes discomfort to every pure conscience.

Here the following questions arise:

1. Is the Prophet of Islam (s) pleased with these circumstances or not?
2. Why we have become like this?
3. What is the solution?
4. Who is responsible?

Complete answers of the above questions require detailed explanation, but here we would be content with only brief and condensed replies:

Is the Prophet of Islam pleased with these circumstances?

No Muslim, having insight would deny that the present dire circumstances of the Muslim world are not satisfactory for the Prophet of Islam (s). How can the Prophet of Islam (s) be pleased that his community should remain under the domination of infidelity and hegemony? And the Islamic lands should be under the exploitation and usurpation of infidels and that their Muslim owners should be rendered homeless? How he can be satisfied that his Ummah should surrender its natural resources to the enemies of Islam at such a paltry cost and after that they have to beg the same enemies for help and assistance? Or that they deprive their own people from the basic necessities in order to use welfare funds for financing the arms race and purchase of destructive weapons, which are sometimes also used against neighboring countries.

No, the Prophet of Islam (s) can never be satisfied with these tragic and degrading circumstances and he does not like his Ummah to be in such a condition.

Why have we become like this?

This has happened, because we have not acted on the commands of Islam and Quran, because Quran considers all Muslims to be a single community and it says:

"And hold fast by the covenant of Allah all together and be not disunited." (3:103)

"And obey Allah and His Apostle and do not quarrel for then you will be weak in hearts and your power will depart, and be patient; surely Allah is with the patient." (8:46)

"..and Allah will by no means give the unbelievers a way

against the believers." (4:141)

"Those who take the unbelievers for guardians rather than believers. Do they seek honor from them? Then surely all honor is for Allah." (4:139)

But Muslims become friendly to the infidels in order to gain honor and power and open venues of their exploitation and domination.
Quran says:

"O you who believe! do not take the unbelievers for friends rather than the believers; do you desire that you should give to Allah a manifest proof against yourselves?" (4:144)
It has also said:

"O you who believe! do not take the Jews and the Christians for friends; they are friends of each other; and whoever amongst you takes them for a friend, then surely he is one of them; surely Allah does not guide the unjust people." (5:51)

But Muslims have violated the clear and absolute commands of Quran and gave to the deadly enemies of Islam, oaths of friendship and cooperation in the fields of administration, economics, culture and politics. Quran says:

"...and fight the polytheists all together as they fight you all together, and know that Allah is with those who guard (against evil). (9:36)

In the same way, it says:

"...then fight the leaders of unbelief - surely their oaths are nothing - so that they may desist." (9:12)

But Muslims have abandoned the important duty of Jihad and chosen a life of degradation over Jihad and honorable martyrdom in the way of God and instead of Jihad, they form pacts of friendship and cooperation.

The Holy Quran says:

"And from among you there should be a party who invite to good and enjoin what is right and forbid the wrong, and these it is that shall be successful." (3:104)

But Muslims have omitted the important duty of 'Enjoining good and forbidding evil' and as a result of it, have sold themselves to the mischief makers and rulers and oppressors have gained control on them as a result of which, social and moral corruptions have gained popularity.

In addition to that we have not fulfilled numerous human and religious duties and as a result of that we have become involved in bad circumstances. Therefore, the present circumstances are the result of our role.

Abu Huraira says: I heard the Messenger of Allah (s) say to Thauban: O Thauban, what will you do when communities would invite cooperation of each other in gaining domination over you, just as you call each other to dinner spread? Thauban said: O Messenger of Allah (s), is it due to the paucity of our numbers? He replied: No, on that day you would be in large numbers. On the contrary, it is as a result of sloth and weakness, which has overpowered you. He asked: O Messenger of Allah (s), what do you mean by sloth. He replied: Love of the world and dislike of fighting.[209]

The Messenger of Allah (s) said: As long as two kinds of negligences do not appear among you, you will have proof and guide from Almighty Allah: One is intoxication of ignorance and secondly intoxication with attachment to life. As long as you are not involved in these two things and continue 'Enjoining of good and forbidding evil' and perform Jihad in the way of God, you would be guided by Almighty Allah, but when you become infatuated with the world and neglect 'Enjoining of good and forbidding evil' and Jihad in the way of God, on that day, those who had been faithful to the Book and Sunnah and called the people to them will be in the rank of the first believers among Emigrants (Muhajireen) and Helpers (Ansar).[210]

Abu Huraira has narrated from the Messenger of Allah (s) that he said: 'Enjoin good and forbid evil', otherwise Almighty Allah would make evil and mischievous persons dominant over you. At that time, the righteous would supplicate, but their supplications would not be answered.[211]

What is the solution?

The only solution of this problem is that we should return to true Islam; that we revive the original, life giving and motivating values among us; that we invite the disunited Muslims to unity and formation

---

[209] Majmauz Zawaid, Vol. 7, Pg. 287

[210] Majmauz Zawaid, Vol. 7, Pg. 270

[211] Majmauz Zawaid, Vol. 7, Pg. 266

of a single community. We should revive the philosophy of Jihad, martyrdom and enjoining of good and forbidding of evil and defense of religion and Islamic lands. We should confront the tyrants and their followers and supporters. We should halt the progress of foreign domination and enemies of Islam in Islamic countries and we should take initiative to achieve self sufficiency and independence.

Although in the present circumstances, achieving the final aim is a difficult job. It calls for loyalty, sacrifice, bearing imprisonments, tortures, exile, martyrdom and deprivation; but we have no other option. We should move with sincerity and take steps and Almighty Allah will also help:

> *"O you who believe! if you help (the cause of) Allah, He will help you and make firm your feet." (47:7)*

Amirul Momineen (a) said: If you face difficulty and hardships, spend your wealth and if a difficulty appears for your religion, sacrifice your life in defense of religion. You should know that destroyed is the one, who loses his faith and in loss is one, whose faith has been stolen. You should know that after Paradise, there is no poverty and in the presence of Hell fire there is no wealth; and that also a fire, which does not allow any of its captives to escape and the one diseased by it, is never cured.[212]

Who is responsible?

All of us are responsible, because the obligation of defending religion is a universal responsibility. Every person, in all conditions, can help in achieving this important aim. But intellectuals, reformers,

---

[212] Wasailush Shia, Vol. 16, Pg. 192

jurisprudents and scholars of religion have more responsibility to it; they are supposed to invite people to unity, propagate original and forgotten values of Islam, expose the dangerous conspiracies of the enemies, take up the leadership of the community and prepare Muslims to defend Islam, to establish religion and to apply perfect laws. They should themselves become fully active and also take people with them.

Amirul Momineen (a) said: "Behold, by Him who split the grain (to grow) and created living beings, if people had not come to me and supporters had not exhausted the argument and if there had been no pledge of Allah with the learned to the effect that they should not acquiesce in the gluttony of the oppressor and the hunger of the oppressed, I would have cast the rope of Caliphate on its own shoulders."[213]

Imam Husain (a) also said: Moreover, the courses of affairs and rulings are under the control of the scholars, who are the keepers of the legal and the illegal affairs of God. This standing is surely seized from you just because you have gone in different direction away from the right and disagreed about the Sunnah after the clear exposition of the evidences. If you tolerated the harm and bore the burdens for God's sake, all the affairs of God would arrive at your hands, emanate from you, and devolve upon you.

But you have made the unjust rulers occupy your positions and handed over the affairs of God to them. They are acting suspiciously and pursuing their passions. Your escape from death and adherence to this life, which will sooner or later leave you, gave them a free hand on doing so. Thus, you forsook the weak ones, some of whom were enslaved compulsorily and others were suffering under the control of the straits of livelihood. The unjust rulers therefore are rolling in royalty with their own opinions and disgracing others by their

---

[213] Nahjul Balagha, Sermon 3

own passions as they follow the examples of the evil and dare the All-omnipotent (God). In every country, they are assigning an eloquent orator on the pulpits of God. Lands are vacant for them as their hands are prevailing upon everything and people are taken as their slaves, because they lack the power to defend themselves. They are either a transgressing tyrant or a domineering, coarse to the weak, and obeyed who does not acknowledge the Initiator, the Recreator. How strange this is! I should be astonished at such affairs, when the lands are prevailed upon by tyrannical cheaters, wrongful bribers or unmerciful governors. God is the judge in our question of disputation and His judgment will pass over our controversy.[214]

Yes, well wishers and scholars of religion are duty bound to take over the leadership of the community and to wave the standard of defense of religion and Islamic values in the world and guide Islam and Muslims on the way of God. If efforts and struggle of all begin, it is hoped that with the help and support of God, the lost glory and honor of Islamic community would return and it would obtain its own position in the world.

Fortunately, signs of Islamic revival are apparent in the world and it is necessary to take advantage of this very sensitive situation.

Zakat

Zakat

The Almighty Allah, in order to fulfill the needs of the poor, has placed a share of poor in the wealth of the rich, which in Islamic

---

[214] Tohafful Uqool, Pg. 242

terminology is named as Zakat. Zakat is a religious obligation, which is much emphasized in verses of Quran and traditions of the Prophet. So much so, that it is mentioned alongside Prayers:

> *"And keep up prayer and pay the poor-rate and bow down with those who bow down." (2:43)*

> *"And keep up prayer and pay the poor-rate and whatever good you send before for yourselves, you shall find it with Allah; surely Allah sees what you do." (2:110)*

> *"...and (as for) those who hoard up gold and silver and do not spend it in Allah's way, announce to them a painful chastisement." (9:34)*

We also have numerous traditions about Zakat and some of them are as follows:

> *Imam Muhammad Baqir (a) said: Almighty Allah has mentioned Zakat alongside Prayers in Quran and said: "**Establish Prayer and pay the Zakat.**" Thus, all those who pray and do not pay Zakat are as if they have not even recited the prayers.[216]*

Imam Ja'far Sadiq (a) said: Allah has not made anything obligatory on the Islamic Ummah, which is more difficult than Zakat and most people would be sent to Hell on this pretext only.[217]

In the same way, he said: One, who refrains from paying Zakat to the extent of one carat, is not Muslim and he would die the death of either Judaism or Christianity.[218]

Imam Muhammad Baqir (a) said: One who does not pay the Zakat of his wealth, Almighty Allah would impose it in the form of a huge serpent of fire on his neck and till the accounting is complete, it would continue to bite him and it was regarding this that Allah, the Mighty and Sublime said: "...they shall have that whereof they were niggardly made to cleave to their necks on the resurrection day..."[219]

Imam Ja'far Sadiq (a) said: Zakat became obligatory so that the wealthy are tested and they become means of livelihood for the poor. If people pay the Zakat of their wealth, no poor Muslim would remain; on the contrary, needs of all of them would be fulfilled through Zakat. Thus the presence of poor, needy, hungry and naked among the people is due to the sin of the wealthy. It is right for Allah, the Mighty and the High, to prevent His mercy from those who does not pay the rightful share of Allah from their wealth.[220]

Amirul Momineen (a) said: "Then, Zakat has been laid down along with prayer as a sacrifice (to be offered) by the people of Islam. Whoever pays it by way of purifying his spirit, it serves as a purifier for him and a protection and shield against fire (of Hell). No one therefore (who pays it) should feel attached to it afterwards, nor should feel grieved over it. Whoever pays it without the intention of purifying his heart, expects through it more than his due. He is certainly ignorant of the Sunnah, he is allowed no reward for it, his action goes to waste and his repentance is excessive."[221]

His Eminence, Imam Musa Ibne Ja'far (a) said: Guard your wealth through payment of Zakat.[222]

1. After Prayers, Zakat is the most important command of Islam. Therefore, in the Holy Quran, it is mentioned after Prayers. Thus one who does not pay the Zakat of his wealth, his Prayers will also not be accepted and he will not depart from the world as a Muslim, on the contrary, he dies the death of a Jew or a Christian.

2. Zakat has been made obligatory so that the wealthy may be tested, because paying of their wealth and that also with their pleasure and sincerity is a difficult job.
3. Zakat has been legislated to fulfill the needs of the life of poor.
4. If Zakat is paid in the right and complete manner and is distributed, no more hungry and naked ones would be seen.
5. By paying Zakat, there is increase in wealth and it remains safe.
6. Paying Zakat is one of the best worship acts, which if fulfilled with intention of proximity and sincerity, would serve as a means of divine proximity and penalty for sins.

Items on which Zakat is payable

Zakat is an Islamic tax, which is applicable on the wealth of the affluent people. The Muslim ruler, from the side of Allah, is responsible to collect it from the rich and to spend it in fulfilling the needs of the poor. The Holy Quran says:

> *"Take alms out of their property, you would cleanse them and purify them thereby and pray for them; surely your prayer is a relief to them; and Allah is Hearing, Knowing." (9:103)*

The Messenger of Allah (s) fully used this command and according to the conditions of Muslim, applied taxes on the wealth of the rich, which is applicable to nine things and in collecting Zakat, he overlooked all secondary taxes.

Those nine items are as follows: camels, cows, goats and sheep [who graze in natural pastures and not on private lands]. Gold and silver coins (dirhams and dinar, which was the currency of that period), subject to the condition that its taxable quantity is owned by a person for 11 months continuously; wheat, barley, dates and resins.

Imam Ja'far Sadiq (a) said: When the following verse was revealed in the month of Ramadhan: "Take alms out of their property, you would cleanse them and purify them thereby...," the Messenger of Allah (s) ordered his announcer to announce in public that just as Allah, the Mighty and the High has made Prayers obligatory, He has also made Zakat obligatory. Thus, pay Zakat on gold, silver, camels, cows, sheep, wheat, barley, dates and resins. But he allowed the rest to remain with them.[223]

It is narrated from Imam Muhammad Baqir and Imam Ja'far Sadiq (a) that they said: Allah has made Zakat obligatory along with Prayers. Thus the Messenger of Allah (s) fixed it for nine items; and he overlooked the rest: gold, silver, camels, cows, sheep, wheat, barley, dates and resins.[224]

These things were the most important sources of income for the Muslims of that time, which the Messenger of Allah (s) subjected for payment of Zakat, and by collecting and spending it, he fulfilled the needs of the poor and deprived to an extent.

But, in the present age aeroplanes, ships and automobiles have replaced camels as mode of conveyance. Cows and sheep who graze on natural pastures and which come under the condition of Zakat are very less and it is replaced by animal husbandry and poultry industry on a large scale. Now, we have no more gold and silver coinage, which might be saved, on the contrary in their place, paper currency and the like have appeared. These days, rice is the staple food of most people and it grows in abundance.

Finally, in a time when the quantum of Zakat on wheat, barley, dates and resins after deduction of the heavy costs that it entails, is insufficient to pay the cost of living of the poor and needy; in such circumstances and conditions what the value of Zakat will be and how it would defray the cost of living of needy, deprived, helpless aged and children without guardians etc.? Definitely, Islam in this regard has displayed foresight and there are various options. Therefore, it is necessary for the Muslim jurists and scholars to derive means of incomes from sources of Islamic laws and to present them to the Islamic government authorities.

Disposal of Zakat

The Muslim authority collects Zakat from the wealthy and spends it in the following ways:

1. It may be given to a poor person, who does not possess actual or potential means to meet his own expenses, as well as that of his family for a period of one year. However, a person who has an art or possesses property or capital to meet his expenses is not classified as poor.

2. It may be paid to a destitute person (Miskeen), who leads a harder life than a poor person (Faqeer).

3. It can be given to an indebted person, who is unable to repay his debt.

4. It may be given to a stranded traveler.

5. It may be spent in the way of Allah for things, which have common benefit to the Muslims; for example, to construct a mosque, or a school for religious education, or to keep the city clean, or to widen or to build tar roads or to publish books.

6. It can be given to a person who is a representative (Wakil) of the Imam or his representative to collect Zakat, to keep it in safe custody, to maintain its accounts and to deliver it to the Imam or his representative or to the poor.

7. It can be given to those non-Muslims, who may, as a result, be inclined to Islam, or may assist the Muslims with the Zakat for fighting against the enemies, or for other justified purposes. It can be given to those Muslims also, whose faith in the Prophet or in the Wilayat of Amirul Momineen is unstable and weak, provided that, as a result of giving, their faith is entrenched.

8. It can be spent to purchase slaves to set them free.

The Holy Quran says:

> *"Alms are only for the poor and the needy, and the officials (appointed) over them, and those whose hearts are made to incline (to truth) and the (ransoming of) captives and those in debts and in the way of Allah and the wayfarer; an ordinance from Allah; and Allah is knowing, Wise." (9:60)*

With attention to the above tradition, the legislation of Zakat was effected so that the above expenditures may be taken care of.[225]

---

[216] Wasailush Shia, Vol. 9, Pg. 22
  [217] Wasailush Shia, Vol. 9, Pg. 28
  [218] Wasailush Shia, Vol. 9, Pg. 32
  [219] Wasailush Shia, Vol. 9, Pg. 22
  [220] Wasailush Shia, Vol. 9, Pg. 12
  [221] Nahjul Balagha, Sermon 199
  [222] Wasailush Shia, Vol. 9, Pg. 11
  [223] Wasailush Shia, Vol. 9, Pg. 53
  [224] Wasailush Shia, Vol. 9, Pg. 55
  [225] For more details about laws of Zakat, see books of jurisprudence.

Khums

Khums

Khums is also an obligatory tax, which is collected from the properties of the rich. Its quantity is one-fifth of the profit of man after all expenses have been paid and it is applicable on seven items:

1. Spoils of war.
2. Minerals, after paying the expenses of taking them out.
3. Treasure trove.
4. Gems obtained from sea diving.
5. Profit or gain from earning, after one has paid his and his family's expenses from it.
6. A land, which a Zimmi (a non-Muslim living under the protection of Islamic Government) purchases from a Muslim.
7. When lawful (Halaal) wealth is mixed with unlawful (Haraam) and their quantum is not known.

One who obtains any of the above; it is obligatory on him or her to pay its Khums to the religious authority in Islam, so that he may spend it in the ways fixed for it.

The Holy Quran says:

> *"And know that whatever thing you gain, a fifth of it is for Allah and for the Apostle and for the near of kin and the orphans and the needy and the wayfarer, if you believe in Allah and in that which We revealed to Our servant, on the day of distinction, the day on which the two parties met; and Allah has power over all things." (8:41)*

"Whatever thing you gain" literally means that, which a person earns without working for it. In Qamus, it is mentioned that all variations of this word imply: Wealth, which a person obtains without working for it.

Raghib has written that 'Mughnam' (gain) is something, which a person gets as booty.

It is mentioned in Al-Munjid that: 'Ghanimat' (gain) is a thing, which is confiscated from the enemies through use of force and it basically means 'income'.

Allamah Tabatabai says: 'Ghanim' and 'Ghaneemat' (gain) is used in the meaning of earning profits made through business, employment or fighting battles. But in the context of revelation of the verse, it implies war booty.[215]

On the basis of this, although the verse was revealed with regard to the Battle of Badr, it has other implications as well and its meaning is not restricted. Therefore, it includes every kind of income, especially with attention to the term of 'whatever thing', as is generally apparent. The same meaning is hinted at in some traditions as well.

> *Imam Ja'far Sadiq (a) has narrated from his forefathers that the Holy Prophet (s) said in his bequest to Ali Ibne Abi Talib (a): O Ali, Abdul Muttalib, during the period of ignorance, acted on five practices, which Allah, the Mighty and the High, continued in Islam: (till he said) when Abdul Muttalib obtained a treasure trove, he took out Khums from it and donated it to charity; thus Almighty Allah revealed the following verse:* **"And know that whatever thing you gain, a fifth of it is for Allah..."**[216]

Imam Muhammad Baqir (a) wrote to Ali bin Mahziyar: Thus, windfalls and profits of every year are obligatory on them, as Allah, the Mighty

---

[215] Al-Mizan, Vol. 9, Pg. 89

[216] Wasailush Shia, Vol. 9, Pg. 496

and the High has said: "And know that whatever thing you gain, a fifth of it is for Allah and for the Apostle and for the near of kin and the orphans and the needy and the wayfarer, if you believe in Allah and in that which We revealed to Our servant, on the day of distinction, the day on which the two parties met; and Allah has power over all things."

Thus 'Ghanaim' (gains) is the same profit and booty, which a person obtains and it is inheritance, which he receives from strangers and the enemy, who after surrendering to him pays him and also the property, whose owner is unknown.[217]

Samaa-a says: I asked His Eminence, Imam Musa Ibne Ja'far (a) about Khums. He replied: It is on anything, which a person gets, whether it is less or more.[218]

On the basis of this, the 'obigatori-ness' of Khums is not restricted to war booties, on the contrary, it is applicable to all incomes, including income from business and salaries.

Disposal of Khums

Disposal of Khums is on the same six instances, which are mentioned in the verse: God, the Messenger of God (s), relatives, orphans, poor and the stranded traveler.

The Messenger of Allah (s) takes three shares from the above six: Share of God, share of Messenger and share of relatives. [Relatives in tradition are interpreted as the infallible Imams as they were relatives of the Messenger of Allah (s)] In this way, he paid for his expenses as well as his family members and whatever remained in excess, he spent it on the common Muslims. He spent the other three shares (Saadaat[219] orphans, poor and stranded travelers) in the proper manner as well,

---

[217] Wasailush Shia, Vol. 9, Pg. 501

[218] Wasailush Shia, Vol. 9, Pg. 503

[219] A Sayyid or a descendant of Lady Fatima Zahra (s) through Imam Husain (a)

since he was the authority and ruler of Muslims.

It is concluded from traditions that after the Messenger of Allah (s) the total amount of Khums was placed under the charge of Ali Ibne Abi Talib (a) and his eleven descendants, who are successors of the Prophet and lawful rulers of Islam, that they might spend it in the way as the Messenger of Allah (s) used to spend.

Ahmad has narrated from Ahmad Ibne Muhammad Ibne Abu Nasr, who has said the following. "Once a person asked Imam Reza (a) about the words of Allah, the Most Majestic, the Most gracious, "Know that whatever property you may gain, one fifth belongs to God, the Messenger, the kindred..." (8:41) It then was asked, "The portion that belongs to Allah to who does it go?" The Imam (a) said, "It belongs to the Messenger of Allah and whatever belongs to the Messenger of Allah, belongs to the Imam."

Another question said, "If one of the categories of welfare recipient would be more and the other category less, then how is it dealt with?" The Imam (a) said, "It is left to the discretion of the Imam consider how the Messenger of Allah dealt with such cases. Is it not the case that he used his own discretion and distributed as he considered proper? The Imam would deal with such case in the same way."[220]

On the basis of this, the total amount of Khums is the right of God, which is related to the wealth of the wealthy and Holy Infallibles (a) spent it in the above manner.

> *Muhammad Ibne Muslim has narrated from Abu Ja'far, Imam Muhammad Baqir (a) who has said the following with regard to the words of Allah, the Most High.* **"Know that whatever property you may gain, one fifth belongs to God, the Messenger, the kindred..." (8:41)** *"It refers to the relatives of the Messenger of*

---

[220] Al-Kafi, Vol. 1, Pg. 544

Allah. Khums (one fifth) belongs to Allah, the Messenger and to us."[221]

Imran bin Musa has quoted Imam Musa Ibne Ja'far (a) that he said with regard to the verse of Khums: Share of God is placed at the discretion of the Messenger of Allah (s) and that which belongs to the Messenger of Allah (s) is related to us.[222]

On the basis of this, according to the belief of Imamite Shia, in the present age, Khums has to be paid to the twelfth Imam, His Eminence, Hujjat Ibnul Hasan Askari (a), but regretfully no access is available to his holy being.

Now, the question arises that what is the duty of Khums during the period of occultation of Imam Zamana (a)?

This matter has been studied in detail in books of jurisprudence and different views are explained. Finally, it is concluded that during the period of occultation, Khums should be paid to the Islamic jurisprudent (Faqih), who is having all the necessary qualifications, as he is having authority on Muslims and is the leader of Islamic community. The administration of religious colleges is also under his charge. He spends the amount of Khums in glorifying the word of monotheism, propagating sciences and beliefs of Islam, defense of Islam and Quran, establishment of judiciary and executive of laws of religion, Islamic colleges, fulfilling needs of poor Saadaat, because spending of Khums in these instances will definitely be according to the pleasure of Imam Zamana (a).

---

[221] Al-Kafi, Vol. 1, Pg. 539

[222] Wasailush Shia, Vol. 9, Pg. 516

Bibliography

1. Aamadi, Abdul Wahid, Ghurarul Hikam, Second Edition, Darul Kitab Islami, Qom 1410.
2. Ibne Kathir, Ali bin Abil Karam, Usudul Ghaba, Intisharaat Ismailiyan, Tehran, [Undated]
3. Ibne Hisham, As-Seeratun Nabawiyyah, Matba Mustafa Baati, Egypt, 1355
4. Abul Fida Ismail bin Kathir, Al-Bidaya wan Nihaya, First Edition, Daar Ahya Thurathul Arabiyya, Beirut, 1408 A.H.
5. Ahmad bin Hanbal, Musnad, Daar Saadir, Beirut, [Undated]
6. Bukhari, Muhammad bin Ismail, Sahih Bukhari, Daar Ahya Kutubul Arabiyya
7. Tirmidhi, Muhammad bin Isa bin Surah, Al-Jamiul Sahih, Daar Ahya Thurathul Arabi, Beirut
8. Tustari, Muhammad Taqi, Qamusur Rijal, Markaz Nashr Kitab, Tehran, 1340
9. Juwaini, Ibrahim bin Muhammad, Faraidus Simtain, First Edition, Mausisa Mahmoodi, Beirut, 1400
10. Hakim Nishaburi, Abu Abdullah, Al-Mustadrak Alaa Sahihain,

Maktabul Matbuaat Islamiya, Beirut

11. Harani, Hasan bin Ali bin Husain, Tohafful Uqul, Kitab Faroshi Islamiya, Tehran 1384 A.H.

12. Hurre Amili, Muhammad bin Hasan, Wasailush Shia, First Edition, Mausisa Aale Bayt, Qum, 1409 A.H.

13. Khatib Baghdadi, Ahmad bin Ali, Tarikh Baghdad, Daarul Kitabul Arabi, Beirut, [Undated]

14. Khawarizmi, Maufaq bin Ahmad, Al-Manaqib, Maktabatul Haidariyya, Najaf 1385

15. Raghib Isfahani, Hasan bin Muhammad, Al-Mufradat, Al-Maktabatul Murtazwiya, Tehran

16. Shaykh Hurre Amili, Muhammad bin Hasan, Athbatul Huda, Matba Ilmiya, Tehran

17. Subhi Salih, Nahjul Balagha, Darul Hijra, Qom

18. Tabarsi, Ali, Mishkatul Anwaar, Maktabatul Haidariyya, Najaf 1385

19. Tabarsi, Fazl bin Hasan, Majmaul Bayan, Fifth Edition, Kitab Faroshi Islamiya, Tehran 1395 A.H.

20. Aliyyar, Mulla Ali, Bahjatul Amaal, Buniyad Farhang Kushanpour

21. Faiz Kashani, Mulla Mohsin, Al-Haqaiq, Maktabatul Islamiyya 1378

22. The Holy Quran

23. Qunduzi, Sulaiman, Ibrahim, Yanabiul Mawaddah, Seventh Edition, Maktabatul Haidariyya, Najaf 1384

24. Katani, Abdul Hayy, At-Tarateebul Idariya, Daar Ahya Thurathul Arabiyya, Beirut, [Undated]

25. Kulaini, Muhammad bin Yaqub, Al-Kafi, Daarul Kutub Islamiyya, Tehran, 1388 A.H.

26. Majlisi, Allamah Muhammad Baqir, Biharul Anwar, Al-Maktabatul Islamiyya, Tehran, 1386 A.H.

27. Muizzi, Ismail, Jamiul Ahadith Shia, First Edition, Tehran, 1379

A.H.

28. Noori Tabarsi, Mirza Husain, Mustadrakul Wasail, Mausisa Aale Bayt Li Ahya Turath, Qom, 1407

29. Nishaburi, Muslim bin Hajjaj, Sahih Muslim, Second Edition, Daar Ahya Thurathul Arabiyya, Beirut, [Undated]

30. Haithami, Ahmad bin Hijr, As-Sawaiqul Mohriqa, Second Edition, Maktabatul Qahira, Cairo, Beirut, [Undated]

31. Haithami, Ali bin Abi Bakr, Majmauz Zawaid, Second Edition, Darul Kutubul Arabi, Beirut, 1967 A.D.

www.ingramcontent.com/pod-product-compliance
Lightning Source LLC
LaVergne TN
LVHW041932070526
838199LV00051BA/2781